At Issue

| Student Debt

Other Books in the At Issue Series

At Issue

| Student Debt

Avery Elizabeth Hurt, Book Editor

Published in 2020 by Greenhaven Publishing, LLC
353 3rd Avenue, Suite 255, New York, NY 10010

First Edition

Articles in Greenhaven Publishing anthologies are often edited for length to meet page
requirements. In addition, original titles of these works are changed to clearly present
the main thesis and to explicitly indicate the author's opinion. Every effort is made to
ensure that Greenhaven Publishing accurately reflects the original intent of the authors.
Every effort has been made to trace the owners of the copyrighted material.

Cover image: Cargo/Imagezoo/Getty Images

Library of Congress Cataloging-in-Publication Data

Names: Hurt, Avery Elizabeth, editor.
Title: Student debt / Avery Elizabeth Hurt, book editor.
Other titles: Student debt (Greenhaven Publishing)
Description: First edition | New York : Greenhaven Publishing, 2020. | Series: At
issue | Includes bibliographical references and index. | Audience: Grades 9–12.
Identifiers: LCCN 2019022823 | ISBN 9781534506237 (library
binding) | ISBN 9781534506220 (paperback)
Subjects: LCSH: College costs—United States—Juvenile literature. | Student loans—United
States—Juvenile literature. | Education, Higher—United States—Finance—Juvenile
literature. | Government aid to higher education—United States—Juvenile literature.
Classification: LCC LB2342 .S864 2020 | DDC 378.3/8—dc23
LC record available at https://lccn.loc.gov/2019022823

Manufactured in the United States of America

Website: http://greenhavenpublishing.com

Contents

Introduction

As of this writing, student debt in the United States has topped 1.4 trillion dollars, with more than 40 million people still paying off their student loans. Higher education is now second only to home mortgages when it comes to individual debt. Many of those borrowers are struggling to pay or have even defaulted on those loans. This situation has created a crisis that affects the lives of individuals and families all across the nation.

Funding for public colleges and universities has traditionally come from a combination of state and federal sources. The federal government supports higher education primarily by providing financial assistance to individual students. (The federal government also funds many research projects at universities.) States are generally responsible for the basic operational costs of public colleges. Private colleges, which get no funding from states, depend on donations and endowments, as well as tuition and research grants.

The Great Recession of 2008 led to tremendous cuts in state funding for higher education, as well as a devaluing of endowments at private schools. As a consequence, schools were forced to increase tuition, forcing students to borrow even more money to pay for college. Once the recovery was underway, wages did not recover in keeping with the rest of the economy, making it difficult for many graduates to find jobs that paid enough for them to meet their loan payments.

The problem of college costs, however, predates the Great Recession. Since the 1980s, college tuition has been increasing much faster than other things—even health care—while wages have remained nearly flat. On top of that, student debt is handled much differently than other types of debt, making it more difficult to manage. People who have student loans are exempted from some of the protections afforded to other borrowers. For example, education loans are not (except in exceptional circumstances) dischargeable in bankruptcies. The borrowers also have less recourse for protesting predatory collection practices than do other borrowers.

The federal government provides financial assistance to students by means of a system of grants, work study programs, and a complex system of federally insured loans. For many years, most student loans were "direct" loans, meaning that the government itself provided the loan without involving a private bank. Since 2005, however, there has been a marked increase in the number of private banks offering student loans. Private loans are typically more expensive with less favorable terms than direct loans. Private lenders have also been known to use some shady business tactics. For example, sometimes lenders would attempt to confuse students and their families, making borrowers think they were getting a loan from a federal program rather than a private lender. Private lenders also often loaned students far more than they needed, increasing the students' debt burden. One study, by the Consumer Financial Protection Bureau, found that some of these loans were for 151 percent of the student's tuition.

Aggressive marketing, often targeting students who can't afford these interest rates, has compounded the problem. First generation college students and those who are not familiar with the ins and outs of borrowing made especially rich targets for unscrupulous lenders. The student debt crisis was made significantly worse in recent years by the advent of for-profit colleges. These companies account for almost a third of all student loans and typically cost far more than state universities. For-profit colleges are especially likely to prey on low-income and minority students.

Though the average student loan payment is not excessive, students who do not graduate or cannot find a good-paying job when they graduate often have difficulty paying. Late payments and interest can accumulate, making it increasingly difficult to get ahead of the debt. Students who dropped out of college or went to for-profit colleges are more likely than graduates from state or private universities to be struggling to make their payments.

Getting behind or defaulting on student debt can create a domino effect of consequences, starting with a hit to the individual's credit rating. This can make it difficult to buy a car, which might be necessary for a person to get to work. It can also make it difficult to find a job because many employers refuse to hire people with poor credit. And, of course, if you can't find a job or can't get to work if you have one, then you're not going to be able to make those loan payments. It quickly becomes a downward spiral that is nearly impossible to get out of. For many people, the struggle can last a lifetime. The psychological impact of being deeply in debt and hounded by creditors is tremendous, as well.

Some people manage to pay their loan payments, but those payments eat up so much of their income that don't have enough left to buy homes. They may be hesitant to start families because of their debt. People saddled with student debt often put off marriage or having children until much later than they would have had they been more financially secure. Excessive debt also prevents people from starting businesses or taking other financial risks. These things have lasting effects on individual lives, of course, but also affect the national economy. Millions of people are putting money into paying off loans—money they otherwise would have spent on things that boost the economy.

In 1965, President Lyndon Johnson said, "Poverty must not be a bar to learning, and learning must offer an escape from poverty." For most of the history of this country, education has been the best route out of poverty. However, today many college graduates find themselves facing a lifetime of poverty or near poverty because of the debt they took on to finance their way out of it.

People have proposed many solutions to the crisis. Some plans involve tying loan payments to income. A borrower would not pay a flat rate payment but would pay a percentage of his or her income. This would solve the problem of people who invested in college but could not find a job that allowed them to earn enough to pay off the debt. If a person lost his or her job or suffered a decrease in salary, the loan payment would be adjusted accordingly.

Others have suggested that the government forgive all student debt (and pay off the small percentage that is not government subsidized). This, advocates say, would boost the economy enough to offset the cost. Some argue that even if it didn't help the economy, it's the right thing to do. Several politicians, particularly Bernie Sanders and Elizabeth Warren, have offered detailed policies for making college free for everyone.

The authors of the viewpoints in *At Issue: Student Debt* discuss these issues and more from a wide variety of backgrounds and philosophical—and sometimes personal—perspectives. They disagree on many particulars, including how serious the "crisis" really is. All agree, however, that education is an integral part of the American dream, and our current system for making education widely available is not working, denying that dream to millions of young people.

1

Why Is There a Student Loan Crisis in the United States?

Eric Best

Eric Best is assistant professor of emergency management at Jacksonville State University in Jacksonville, Alabama. He is the author of The Student Loan Mess, *(University of California Press, 2014).*

In the following viewpoint, Eric Best provides background on the US student loan system and explains how it is unique in its scope and design. He compares the US student loan system with similar programs in Australia, England, and Germany and discusses the options and risks facing the US approach to making a college education available to a greater percentage of its population.

The US student loan system is unique in age, size, and scope. Since 1958, the US has had some form of federally sponsored student loan system. Since inception, college and borrowing have become much more popular, and average balances of student loans have also grown. Currently the federal portfolio consists of more than $US1 trillion of debt.

What's worse is it's unclear just how much of that money the government is going to get back. The federal government treats student-loan debts as assets because they can't be discharged under

"Explainer: The US Student Loan Problem and How We Got Here," by Eric Best, *The Conversation*, November 14, 2014. https://theconversation.com/explainer-the-us-student -loan-problem-and-how-we-got-here-32676. Licensed under CC BY-ND 4.0.

normal circumstances. But that assumption is starting to look a tad optimistic. Studies by the New York Federal Reserve Bank show that about a third of borrowers under 30 and in repayment are delinquent.

How Did the Debt Get So Big?

College tuition fees in the US are not strictly regulated, and the system includes public, private, and for-profit universities. This results in a wide range of tuition and fee charges.

There's a cap on federal loans for undergraduates: $US31,000 for dependent students, and $US57,500 for independent students. These limits are larger for graduate students, and these balances can grow larger than the caps if payments are not made.

The federal loan system is designed to make sure qualified students have access to college, but also that they repay their loans to satisfy investors and protect the government.

This is a system that seems to benefit everyone, and while there have been warning calls for decades about the growth of student loan programs and perverse incentives for both students and institutions, student lending in the United States continues to grow.

Student debt is one of the only types of consumer debt where credit ratings and ability to repay are not taken into account. This has led several countries to adopt income contingent repayment plans intended to reduce the repayment burden for graduates who have a tough time in the initial job market.

These programs are a lifeline for many former students but can be a risk to the governments that hold the debt.

How Are Student Loans Managed Elsewhere?

Since 1989 Australia has had a government-funded student loan program. Repayments begin once graduates reach a certain level of income so they only start paying down their debt after they have entered the working world, this is known as an income contingent loan.

This system does not involve commercial interest; instead loans are indexed to inflation. There is no repayment for a current salary of less than about US$46,500, and a maximum of 8% of total income is collected for loan repayment. There is currently about $AU23 billion of student loans owed to the government (about $US20 billion).

Australia is planning a move to bond-rate interest for current and future student loan balances beginning in 2016, more accurately reflecting the cost of borrowing.

According to recent research, about 20% of loan dollars lent today will not be recovered, and this amount may rise depending on the result of proposed reforms or if higher interest rates make it more difficult to pay down principal.

The income contingent loan system in England is younger but is growing more quickly, as England responds to budgetary issues in higher education by raising tuition.

England currently has about £54.4 billion (about $US86.5B) in outstanding obligations according to a study commissioned by the parliament. Its loan program has only been in place since the early 1990s.

The first tuition charges did not occur until 1998. Tuition caps, which were originally £1000 per year in 1998 rose to £3000 in 2004 and £9000 in 2010, a rate since adopted by most institutions.

All graduates are enrolled in an income contingent program. The English system takes up to 9% of income above an income level of about US$33,000 for 30 years. A report from the Business, Innovation and Skills Committee of Parliament estimates that lending losses may be as high as 45%.

Should We Expand Income Contingent Loans?

Although some income contingent programs have been available since 1994 in the United States, the program that is known today as income-based repayment was enacted in 2007 (followed shortly by Pay as You Earn and 2014 IBR for newer graduates). In comparison to Australia and England, the United States has a low income-based repayment adoption rate. Students must qualify for income-based repayment plans, and many do not even attempt the process.

For the most recently tracked cohort that began student loan repayment in 2011—almost all of whom would be eligible for income-based repayment plans if they were to enroll—there is already a 13.7% default rate three years after finishing school. Currently, default is defined as missing payments for more than 270 days.

Overall, the US student lending portfolio is much larger than those of peer nations, and current policy changes largely advocate for the increased adoption of income-based programs for current and former students.

In contrast to the Australian approach of raising interest rates to offset losses, the American program continues to become more forgiving to graduates entering repayment, as income-based repayment programs have fallen from 20% of income in the 1990s to as low as 10% of income today. There are also proposals to reduce interest rates on existing loans.

According to the Congressional Budget Office, student loans will return a profit of about US$135 billion over the next ten years (using FCRA estimates). However, when the same program is analyzed using fair value accounting—which considers additional risk and market interest rates—it projects a loss of up to US$88 billion over the next ten years (and this is too soon to account for many balances that could be forgiven). Considering the extended repayment timelines of many loans, ten years may not be long enough to consider the total costs of these programs. Student loans are not the only type of debt projected to make money under FCRA and lose money under fair value accounting. Federal Housing Administration programs are still bigger than federal student loans, but the student loan portfolio has grown from 20% of the size of FHA programs in 1992 to 60% of the size of FHA programs in 2011. Student loans are considered more profitable than housing programs under FCRA, and projected to lose more than housing programs under fair value.

In all three countries, income contingent repayment programs are popular for students and are likely to stay, despite the costs to government of incomplete repayment.

If these programs result in large costs to their respective governments, it may make sense to begin to return to pre-loan public education systems and have educational costs financed directly by governments, such as the current model in Germany.

While student loan costs can currently be borne by governments, these programs are likely to have growing costs as adoption increases and tuition growth outpaces inflation.

2

A Radical Solution Is Called For

Marshall Steinbaum

Marshall Steinbaum is a senior economist and fellow at the Roosevelt Institute and one of the founders of the Mapping Student Debt project. He is editor of the book After Piketty: The Agenda for Economics and Inequality *(Harvard University Press, 2017).*

Many solutions have been proposed in response to the growing problem of student debt. Probably none, however, are as radical as this one. In the following viewpoint, Marshall Steinbaum argues that cancelling all currently outstanding student debt would have the counterintuitive effect of modestly stimulating the economy by increasing US GDP and slightly lowering unemployment. He then goes on to address common critiques of this approach.

The Levy Institute recently released a research paper I co-wrote with Stephanie Kelton, Scott Fulwiler, and Catherine Ruetschlin that models the macroeconomic impact of cancelling all of the student debt that is currently outstanding in the United States—just over $1.4 trillion, held by between 40 and 50 million borrowers. The federal government would write off the debt for which it itself is the creditor (the majority of outstanding student loans), and it would assume payments on behalf of borrowers for those loans that are held by private lenders. The population's student loan balance would be reduced to zero—a radical solution

"A Radical Solution to the Student Debt Crisis," by Marshall Steinbaum, Roosevelt Institute, February 6, 2018. Reprinted by permission.

to the student debt crisis, but one that deserves serious attention, given the radical scope of the problem.

The paper finds that student debt cancellation would be modestly stimulative to the macroeconomy, increasing annual GDP by $86 to 108 billion per year. It would increase the demand for labor and therefore slightly reduce the unemployment rate. The crucial mechanism driving the macroeconomic results is that the debt currently weighing down the balance sheets of households and individuals would be transferred to the federal government, which is an efficient reallocation from a macroeconomic perspective since it enables households to spend more, provided that the federal government itself is not financially constrained. Since the macroeconomic models we use assume to varying degrees that it is not (a correct assumption, as a previous paper by my Roosevelt colleague J.W. Mason points out), engaging in that fiscal expansion expands output through greater aggregate demand.

This weighs against the traditional terms in which policy solutions to the student debt crisis are debated: that they would be costly and displace spending on other federal programs. Given that student debt worsens household balance sheets, and that weakness is one of the key mechanisms holding back economic growth, it makes sense to expand the terms of the debate to macroeconomics and outside narrow budgetary calculations.

A recent paper by Daniel Herbst lends credence to these macro dynamics by looking at the effect of income-driven repayment (IDR) on microeconomic decisions and household balance sheets. IDR refers to a set of programs that reduce monthly payments on student loans to be a set percentage of income, and in some cases, cancels the outstanding balance after a certain period of making those payments has elapsed. Herbst finds that enrollment in IDR substantially reduces delinquency (as intended), but it also increases repayment rates by better aligning payments with income and ensuring that temporary cash shortages don't cause default. The increase in repayment is evidence against the notion that reducing indebtedness would have a moral hazard effect by inducing borrowers to take on too much debt (or fail to repay the debt they have) in the expectation that it will be cancelled. IDR also increases borrower credit-worthiness and, likely, homeownership.

Given that full cancellation has never been tried, the best options we have for predicting its economic effects are to either examine the impact of the closest analogs to the policy that have actually been attempted (however imperfect), as Herbst's paper does, or model full cancellation in the context of a more general theory. The Levy Institute paper does the latter.

There's no doubt that full student debt cancellation is an ambitious policy—although, I would point out, it amounts to around the same size in net dollar costs to the government as the recent tax giveaway to the rich, although with a very different beneficiary population. Hence, student debt cancellation would have a much better macroeconomic impact. But the reason why such policies of cancelling (or, less ambitiously, refinancing) student debt have been controversial in the past, at least among higher education scholars, is not their expense, nor their purported effect on the macroeconomy—whether positive or negative. Similar policy proposals have faced two main critiques: that they are inequitable and that student debt is not actually burdening the economy, because the education it buys increases earnings for those borrowers. Both of those critiques are much less true than they are commonly believed to be.

New data from the Department of Education illustrates why these critiques are overdrawn, and it underscores the urgent need for debt relief to borrowers, for whom the bargain inherent in student debt has not paid off.

The Racial Dimension of Student Debt and Student Debt Cancellation

One thing that immediately becomes clear upon investigation of the student debt crisis is the extent to which it is a creature of this country's legacy of racial discrimination, segregation, and economic disadvantage patterned by race. My prior research with Kavya Vaghul found that zip codes with higher population percentages of racial minorities had far higher delinquency rates, and that the correlation of delinquency with race was actually most extreme in middle-class neighborhoods. What this tells us is that student debt is intimately bound up with the route to financial stability for racial minorities.

In that work, we ascribe this pattern of disadvantage to four causes: segregation within higher education, which relegates minority students to the worst-performing institutions, discrimination in both credit and labor markets, and the underlying racial wealth gap that means black and Hispanic students have a much smaller cushion of family wealth to fall back on, both to finance higher education in the first place and also should any difficulty with debt repayment arise. The implication is that while higher education is commonly believed to be the route to economic and social mobility, especially by policy-makers, the racialized pattern of the student debt crisis demonstrates how structural barriers to opportunity stand in the way of individual efforts. Insisting that student debt is not a problem amounts to denying this reality.

Looking at the time series of median wealth for households headed by black and white people between the ages of 25 and 40 (what we refer to as "white households" and "black households") in successive waves of the Survey of Consumer Finances (SCF) reveals these racialized patterns. Overall, and as is well-known, black households have far lower levels of wealth than white households, and in percentage terms, their wealth declined far more in the Great Recession and ensuing "recovery" than did the wealth of white households. While student debt has been increasing as a burden on household balance sheets, that worsening pattern is more pronounced for young black households than for young white households. By this measure, the racial wealth gap (the ratio of the median wealth of white households in that age range to the median wealth of black households in that age range) is approximately 12:1 in 2016, whereas in the absence of student debt, that ratio is 5:1.

Moreover, while overall net household wealth levels for the non-rich increased between the 2013 and 2016 waves of the SCF for the first time since the Great Recession did violence to middle-class wealth, rising student debt weighed in the other direction—especially for black households. The time trend is clear: Student debt is increasingly burdening everyone, but that burden disproportionately weighs on black households.

Why? A 2016 paper by Judith Scott-Clayton and Jing Li offers clues, since it tracks the debt loads of black and white graduates with four-year undergraduate degrees. They find that immediately upon graduating, black graduates have about $7,400 more in student debt than their white counterparts. Four years after graduating, that gap increases to $25,000. The crucial difference is simply that white graduates are likely to find a job and start paying down their debt, more-or-less as the system is designed, but black graduates are not—they carry higher balances, go to graduate school (especially at for-profit institutions) and thus accumulate more debt, and subsequently earn no better than whites with undergraduate degrees.

What this suggests is that any given educational credential is less valuable to blacks in a discriminatory labor market (probably because they attended less well-regarded institutions with weaker networks of post-graduate opportunity, and also because even assuming they did attend the same institutions as their white counterparts, outcomes for black graduates in the labor market are mediated by racial discrimination). As Scott-Clayton and Li write, "These increases occur alongside evidence of growing racial gaps in college graduates' labor market outcomes, suggesting graduate school may for some students be a response to the weak post-recession labor market." Indeed—credentialization is a particular strategy used to navigate a discriminatory labor market without a cushion of family wealth, and student debt is the residue of that strategy. The assumption that debt-financed educational credentialization represents constructive wealth-building and social mobility thus reflects a failure to comprehend the landscape of race-based economic exclusion.

The Benefits of Student Debt Cancellation Extend Beyond High-Income Borrowers

The reason that debt cancellation is considered to be inequitable is that the largest balances are held by the highest-income borrowers. This is undoubtedly true. But what this observation about the cross-section of debtors obscures is the ways that student debt has crept into the far corners of the economy and "trickled down" the income distribution in the years that the total stock of debt has exploded, i.e. since the mid-2000s—as the charts from successive SCF waves show. The reason for that vast enlargement of the population of borrowers is the worsening labor market. Scarce jobs are allocated to the most credentialed applicants, which triggers a rat race of credentialization, and that rat race is worst for minorities. That young cohorts are better educated than their predecessors should result in higher lifetime earnings, if the "skills gap" mythology that motivated the expansion of the federal student loan programs were true. Instead, more and more expensive credentials result in jobs that pay the same or worse, leading to the escalation of debt loads.

Crucially, thanks to increases in tuition, people who would have graduated with little or no debt had they been born in previous cohorts now take on positive balances. And thanks to credentialization, people who would have entered the labor market without degrees in the past now must obtain them, and thus take on debt, in order to get a job. Both dynamics benefit higher education institutions, discriminatory and predatory credit market participants, and powerful employers, which thrive in a segmented market where a captive population must pass through their tollbooth to get to the middle class. These dynamics increase the share of the population with student loan balances greater than zero. Thus, the distribution of borrowers with those positive balances has changed a great deal as the student debt crisis has intensified—a fact that is ignored by analysis that presupposes the pool of student loan borrowers has remained demographically and economically the same over time.

Student debt used to be a mark of the relatively-rich: something that was necessary only for well-paid professionals who spend a long time obtaining a lucrative graduate degree that likely pays off in the form of a high and stable salary over a lifetime. What the worsening labor market, credentialization rat race, and withdrawal of state support for public higher education has done is shift the distribution of people with a positive student loan balance toward the poor, or at least, the much-less-rich. It is still true that the highest balances are carried by the highest-income debtors, but debt cancellation would nonetheless benefit a broad swathe of the public—a swathe that has been victimized by misguided labor market policy, which is what the expansion of the federal student loan programs amounts to.

Scott-Clayton recently followed up her 2016 work by examining the 2017 Department of Education's report referred to above. It utilizes two waves of the Beginning Postsecondary Students Survey to analyze how progression through higher education and student loan repayment differs both between the cohort who entered postsecondary education in 1995-1996 and in 2003-2004, and by race. The study finds that the more recent cohort took on substantially more debt and has had a harder time paying it off, thanks to the weaker labor market that the latter cohort graduated into. And crucially, delinquency and default are prevalent among black borrowers, even those who complete their degrees. Scott-Clayton goes so far as to offer projections that the cumulative 20-year student loan default rate for the 2003-2004 cohort will top 40 percent—an eye-opening suggestion, since it would mean that nearly half of the people who take on student debt ultimately can't pay it off.

Conclusion

Collectively, these findings underscore several takeaways that challenge the conventional wisdom about student debt and higher education: simply ensuring completion of a higher education credential does not guarantee successful labor market outcomes, because those deteriorating outcomes for recent cohorts and young workers have nothing to do with their own education. In that context, the result of increasing higher education attainment and rising student debt is simply credentialization. And at a more macro level, the labor market is not characterized by a skills gap. The idea that it was, and that it could be solved by debt-financed higher education credentials, constitutes a macroeconomically significant misdiagnosis and false prescription—one that has been especially detrimental to the interests of minority borrowers, since it cheapens the value of the credentials they rely on to navigate the economy against a background of racial gaps in wealth and social capital. Thus, while complete debt cancellation may appear to be a radical solution, a radical solution is what the status quo requires.

3

The Student Loan Industry Betrays Young Americans

Daniel Rivero

Daniel Rivero is a producer and reporter for WLRN, a South Florida National Public Radio affiliate. He was one of the reporters for Fusion TV's investigative documentary series The Naked Truth.

In the following viewpoint, Daniel Rivero details how the US student debt industry, which was meant to help young Americans get a college education so they could find good jobs and build a stable economic future, has in fact trapped a generation of Americans in debt. Part of the problem, according to this viewpoint, is the political corruption in the private loan and debt collection industry.

Among the 44 million Americans who have amassed our nation's whopping $1.4tn in student loan debt, a call from Navient can produce shivers of dread.

Navient is the primary point of contact, or the "servicer," for more student loans in the United States than any other company, handling 12 million borrowers and $300bn in debt. The company flourished as student loan debt exploded under the Obama administration, and its stock rose sharply after the election of Donald Trump.

But Navient also has more complaints per borrower than any other servicer, according to a Fusion analysis of data. And these

"The Debt Trap: How the Student Loan Industry Betrays Young Americans," by Daniel Rivero, Guardian News and Media Ltd, September 6, 2017. Reprinted by permission.

mounting complaints repeatedly allege that the company has failed to live up to the terms of its federal contracts, and that it illegally harasses consumers. Navient says most of the ire stems from structural issues surrounding college finance—like the terms of the loans, which the federal government and private banks are responsible for—not about Navient customer service.

Yet during a year-long investigation into who profits off of what has become the largest source of American consumer debt, Fusion TV untangled how Navient has positioned itself to dominate the lucrative student loan industry in the midst of this crisis, flexing its muscles in Washington and increasingly across the states. The story of Navient's emerging power is also the story of how an industry built around the idea that education can break down inequities is reinforcing them.

The tension at the center of the current controversy around student loans is simple: should borrowers be treated like any other consumers, or do they merit special service because education is considered a public good?

Often, the most vulnerable borrowers are not those with the largest debt, but low-income students, first-generation students, and students of color—especially those who may attend less prestigious schools and are less likely to quickly earn enough to repay their loans, if they graduate at all.

"There are populations who are borrowing to go to college or ending up without a degree, and ending up with meaningless degrees, and are … worse off than if they had never gone to college to begin with," said Amy Laitinen, of the nonpartisan think tank New America.

Last year, Navient received 23 complaints per 100,000 borrowers, more than twice that of the nearest competitor, according to Fusion's analysis. And from January 2014 to December 2016, Navient was named as a defendant in 530 federal lawsuits. The vast majority were aimed at the company's student loans servicing operations. (Nelnet and Great Lakes, the two other biggest companies in the student loans market, were sued 32 and 14 times over the same period, respectively.)

Many of the complaints and lawsuits aimed at the company relate to its standard practice of auto-dialing borrowers to solicit payments.

Shelby Hubbard says she has long been on the receiving end of these calls as she has struggled to pay down her debt. Hubbard racked up over $60,000 in public and private student loans by the time she graduated from Eastern Kentucky University with a basic healthcare-related degree.

"It consumes my every day," Hubbard said of the constant calls. "Every day, every hour, starting at 8 o'clock in the morning." Unlike mortgages, and most other debt, student loans can't be wiped away with bankruptcy.

These days, Hubbard, 26, works in Ohio as a logistics coordinator for traveling nurses. She's made some loan payments, but her take-home pay is about $850 every two weeks. With her monthly student loan bill at about $700, roughly half her income would go to paying the loans back, forcing her to lean more heavily on her fiance.

"He pays for all of our utilities, all of our bills. Because at the end of the day, I don't have anything else to give him," she said. The shadow of her debt hangs over every discussion about their wedding, mortgage payments, and becoming parents.

The power and reach of the student loan industry stacks the odds against borrowers. Navient doesn't just service federal loans, it has a hand in nearly every aspect of the student loan system. It has bought up private student loans, both servicing them and earning interest off of them. And it has purchased billions of dollars worth of the older taxpayer-backed loans, again earning interest, as well as servicing that debt. The company also owns controversial subsidiary companies such as Pioneer Credit Recovery that stand to profit from collecting the debt of loans that go into default.

And just as banks have done with mortgages, Navient packages many of the private and pre-2010 federal loans and sells them on

Wall Street as asset-backed securities. Meanwhile, it's in the running to oversee the Department of Education's entire student debt web portal, which would open even more avenues for the company to profit from—and expand its influence over—Americans' access to higher education.

The federal government is the biggest lender of American student loans, meaning that taxpayers are currently on the hook for more than $1tn. For years, much of this money was managed by private banks and loan companies like Sallie Mae. Then in 2010, Congress cut out the middlemen and their lending fees, and Sallie Mae spun off its servicing arm into the publicly traded company Navient.

Led by former Sallie Mae executives, Navient describes itself as "a leading provider of asset management and business processing solutions for education, healthcare, and government clients." But it is best known for being among a handful of companies that have won coveted federal contracts to make sure students repay their loans. And critics say that in pursuit of getting that money back, the Department of Education has allowed these companies to all but run free at the expense of borrowers.

"The problem is that these servicers are too big to fail," said Persis Yu, director of the National Consumer Law Center's Student Loan Borrower Assistance Project. "We have no place to put the millions of borrowers whom they are servicing, even if they are not doing the servicing job that we want them to do."

In its last years, the Obama administration tried to rein in the student loan industry and promoted more options for reduced repayment plans for federal loans. Since then, Donald Trump's education secretary, Betsy DeVos, has reversed or put on hold changes the former education secretary John B. King's office proposed and appears bent on further loosening the reins on the student loan industry, leaving individual students little recourse amid bad service.

In late August, DeVos's office announced that it would stop sharing information about student loan servicer oversight with the federal consumer watchdog agency known as the Consumer Financial Protection Bureau, or CFPB.

Earlier this year, as complaints grew, the CFPB sued Navient for allegedly misleading borrowers about the repayment options it is legally obligated to provide.

A central allegation is that Navient, rather than offering income-based repayment plans, pushed some people into a temporary payment freeze called forbearance. Getting placed into forbearance is a good Band-Aid but can be a terrible longer-term plan. When an account gets placed in forbearance, its interest keeps accumulating, and that interest can be added to the principal, meaning the loans only grow.

Lynn Sabulski, who worked in Navient's Wilkes-Barre, Pennsylvania, call center for five months starting in 2012, said she experienced first-hand the pressure to drive borrowers into forbearance.

"Performing well meant keeping calls to seven minutes or under," said Sabulski. "If you only have seven minutes, the easiest option to put a borrower in, first and foremost, is a forbearance." Sabulski said if she didn't keep the call times short, she could be written up or lose her job.

Navient denies the allegations, and a spokeswoman told Fusion via email seven and a half minutes was the average call time, not a target. The company maintains "caller satisfaction and customer experience" are a significant part of call center representatives' ratings.

But in a 24 March motion it filed in federal court for the CFPB's lawsuit, the company also said: "There is no expectation that the servicer will act in the interest of the consumer." Rather, it argued, Navient's job was to look out for the interest of the federal government and taxpayers.

Navient does get more per account when the servicer is up to date on payments, but getting borrowers into a repayment plan also has a cost because of the time required to go over the complex options.

The same day the CFPB filed its lawsuit, Illinois and Washington filed suits in state courts. The offices of attorneys general in nine other states confirmed to Fusion that they are investigating the company.

At a recent hearing in the Washington state case, the company defended its service: "The State's claim is not, you didn't help at all, which is what you said you would do. It's that, you could've helped them more." Navient insists it has forcefully advocated in Washington to streamline the federal loan system and make the repayment process easier to navigate for borrowers.

And it's true, Navient, and the broader industry, have stepped up efforts in recent years to influence decision makers. Since 2014, Navient executives have given nearly $75,000 to the company's political action committee, which has pumped money mostly into Republican campaigns, but also some Democratic ones. Over the same timespan, the company has spent more than $10.1m lobbying Congress, with $4.2m of that spending coming since 2016. About $400,000 of it targeted the CFPB, which many Republican lawmakers want to do away with.

Among the 22 former federal officials who lobby for Navient is the former US representative Denny Rehberg, a Republican, who once criticized federal aid for students as the welfare of the 21st century. His fellow lobbyist and former GOP representative Vin Weber sits on a board that has aired attack ads against the CFPB, as well as on the board of the for-profit college ITT Tech, which shuttered its campuses in 2016 after Barack Obama's Department of Education accused it of predatory recruitment and lending.

In response to what they see as a lack of federal oversight, California, Connecticut, Massachusetts, and the District of Columbia recently required student loan servicers to get licenses in their states. Not surprisingly, Fusion found a sharp increase in Navient's spending in states considering such regulations, with the majority of the $300,000 in Navient state lobbying allocated since 2016.

In Maine and Illinois, the legislatures were flooded with Navient and other industry lobbyists earlier this year, after lawmakers proposed their own versions of the license bills. The Maine proposal failed after Navient argued the issue should be left to the federal government. The Illinois bill passed the legislature, but the Republican governor, Bruce Rauner, vetoed it in August following lobbying from an industry trade group. Rauner said the bill encroached on the federal government's authority.

Researchers argue more data would help them understand how to improve the student loan process and prevent more people from being overwhelmed by debt. In 2008, Congress made it illegal for the Department of Education to make the data public, arguing that it was a risk for student privacy. Private colleges and universities lobbied to restrict the data. So, too, did Navient's predecessor, Sallie Mae, and other student loan servicing companies.

Today, companies like Navient have compiled mountains of data about graduations, debt and financial outcomes—which they consider proprietary information. The lack of school-specific data about student outcomes can be life-altering, leading students to pick schools they never would have picked. Nathan Hornes, a 27-year-old Missouri native, racked up $70,000 in student loans going to Everest College, an unaccredited school, before he graduated.

"Navient hasn't done a thing to help me," Hornes told Fusion. "They just want their money. And they want it now."

Hornes' loans were recently forgiven following state investigations into Everest's parent company Corinthian. But many other borrowers still await relief.

Better educating teens about financial literacy before they apply to college will help reduce their dependence on student loans, but that doesn't change how the deck is stacked for those who need them. A few states have made community colleges free, reducing the need for student loan servicers.

But until the Department of Education holds industry leaders like Navient more accountable, individual states can fix only so much, insists Senator Elizabeth Warren, one of the industry's most outspoken critics on Capitol Hill.

"Navient's view is, hey, I'm just going to take this money from the Department of Education and maximize Navient's profits, rather than serving the students," Warren said. "I hold Navient responsible for that. But I also hold the Department of Education responsible for that. They act as our agent, the agent of the US taxpayers, the agent of the people of the United States. And they should demand that Navient does better."

4

Forgiving Debt Is Not the Ideal Solution

Miranda Marquit

Miranda Marquit is a journalist who specializes in writing about business, financial markets, and personal finance. Her work has been featured in Forbes, NPR, USNews, and many other publications.

In a previous viewpoint Marshall Steinbaum made the case for why forgiving all student debt would be good for the economy. In the following viewpoint, Miranda Marquit talks with economists who think the effect on the economy might be quite small. Marquit's sources do agree with Steinbaum that is it morally preferable to wipe out student debt than to give tax breaks to the rich but assert that debt forgiveness is unfair to those who've already paid their loans. A better idea, according to this viewpoint, would be policy changes that would ensure workers earned enough to repay their loans.

What if the entire \$1.5 trillion in outstanding US student loan debt was wiped off the books, no questions asked?

Blanket student loan forgiveness for all Americans is exactly what magazine publisher and editor Katrina vanden Heuvel proposed in a June 19 column for the *Washington Post.*

At first glance, this seems like a good idea. After all, student loan debt is causing millennials' net worth to plummet, and many student borrowers have put off milestones such as homeownership because of their debt.

"Should the US Forgive All \$1.5 Trillion in Student Loan Debt?" by Miranda Marquit, Student Loan Hero, June 21, 2018. Reprinted by permission.

But would it be an economic boon for our country? And what obstacles could come up as a result of massive one-time student loan forgiveness? Let's take a look at some of the ramifications.

The Economic Impact of Massive Student Loan Forgiveness

More than 44 million Americans have student loan debt, so the economic effect of forgiving their outstanding balances could make a difference. That's according to Aaron Swisher, a Democrat running for the US House in Idaho's 2nd Congressional District.

"These folks spend a certain amount of money on their student loan payments each month," said Swisher, who has a background in economics. "Without this debt, they'd be able to spend their money on other things, like cars and homes and entertainment."

Debt cancellation could result in a boost to the US gross domestic product (GDP) of, on average, between $86 billion and $108 billion a year, according to a paper published by the Levy Economics Institute.

Others, though, aren't as optimistic about what complete student loan forgiveness would mean for the economy.

"Something in the neighborhood of $80 billion a year in the economy isn't really that much of a dent when you think about it," said Mark Kantrowitz, an education policy expert and the vice president of research at Savingforcollege.com. "We're talking about a GDP of right around $19 [trillion] or $20 trillion a year."

Another long-term economic concern, said Jason Delisle, a resident fellow at the American Enterprise Institute, deals with taxes.

"There would be some economic gain, yes, but at the same time, what if the government has to borrow to pay off a portion of it?" Delisle said. "Someone would have to pay for it later, maybe with higher taxes down the road."

Student Loan Forgiveness: Morality and Fairness

Adam Minsky, a student loan lawyer, agreed that there would be some economic benefit in large-scale student loan forgiveness. But he pointed out that the justification for it might not be there.

"There are other issues at play here, including the morality of it," Minsky said. "You have to look at some of the fairness issues and what this means for students in the future."

While Swisher, the Idaho candidate, acknowledged the potential economic and personal financial benefits of wholesale student loan forgiveness, he still doesn't think it's a good idea. "Morally, if you take on a debt, I think you should pay it," he said.

However, Swisher added that "if you're going to compare policy issues, it's morally better to forgive $1.5 trillion in student debt than to give the wealthy a tax break that will cost us more than $1 trillion in the next 10 years."

Delisle pointed out that many of those with student loans make efforts to repay their debt early, and it's not fair to penalize them. "If you're paying down loans aggressively, working an extra job or postponing a purchase like a car or house, you look like a sucker," he said.

Not only should you repay what you owe, said Beth Akers, a senior fellow at the Manhattan Institute, but you should also look at the policy incentives and whether a one-time student loan forgiveness program is fair to future students.

"First of all, how do you tell students starting college next year that they have to wrack up this debt, but if you had gone four years ago, it would have been free?" said Akers.

Akers went on to suggest that this proposal doesn't address the underlying problems in paying for college. She pointed out that some students might take on more debt than they would have otherwise, hoping to benefit from a similar reprieve in the future. That, in turn, could lead educational institutions to further increase prices, because they would know that people are willing to take on the debt.

So if wiping out all of the student loan debt isn't the answer, what should policymakers do?

Alternatives to Universal Student Loan Forgiveness

There are ways to ease the debt burden on borrowers—without sweeping student loan debt forgiveness.

1. Start with Existing Repayment Programs

Rather than wiping out all of the student debt, Akers said we should start by looking at the programs already in place to help those struggling with student loans.

"Income-driven repayment (IDR) offers a robust system for those who can't afford their payments," said Akers. "We need to help more borrowers understand their options so they can get relief when they can't afford their payments."

Delisle agreed, pointing out that loan forgiveness on an IDR plan is possible after 20 or 25 years. "All of this is done while keeping your payments up to date and without negatively impacting your credit score," he said.

2. Bolster Pell Grants

Rather than forgiving debt after the fact, Kantrowitz would like to see improvements made to the Pell Grant program.

"Research indicates that the Pell Grant increases enrollment and graduation rates," said Kantrowitz. "People would see better-paying jobs and put that [money] back into the economy."

According to Kantrowitz, increasing the amount of the Pell Grant could potentially result in the equivalent of a 14% annualized return on investment over the next 40 years. "There'd be less debt burden and more people able to handle the debt they do have, as well as more in tax revenue," he said.

3. Include Student Loans in Bankruptcy Discharge

"There's no reason for student loan debt to be treated differently than other types of debt," said Minsky. "We don't force people to remain in extreme debt to the detriment of their lives with anything else. Bankruptcy can offer those who need it a fresh start."

Rather than being a free ticket to avoid repaying student loans, Minsky pointed out that there are plenty of deterrents in place when it comes to bankruptcy proceedings. These include a negative impact on your credit, a degree of stigma, and the fact that some types of bankruptcy require additional monthly payments from borrowers.

4. Encourage Livable Wages

A bigger issue is the fact that, even though there's been some recent wage growth, pay has been stagnant for so long that many Americans haven't been able to keep up with inflation, said Swisher. He pointed to a recent report from the National Low Income Housing Coalition illustrating that there's no state in the US where someone working full time on minimum wage can afford a two-bedroom apartment.

"Our economy produces enough that an average worker should be making $100,000 a year," Swisher said. However, he acknowledges that some jobs would clearly pay more than others. "People would be surprised at what should be their share, according to what the economy produces—and if they were getting that, student loan debt wouldn't seem so overwhelming."

What You Can Do About Student Loan Debt

For now, it doesn't look like you can expect massive student loan forgiveness. However, there are steps you can take to reduce your education debt load:

- If you aren't already in college, consider going to a less expensive school and applying for scholarships. Even if you need student loans to close the gap, you won't need to borrow as much.

- Consider refinancing your loans to a lower rate if you have good credit. You might be able to get a more manageable payment and reduce the interest you pay.
- If you can't afford your payments, talk to your loan servicer about getting on an IDR plan.
- Look for side hustles to increase your income. That way, you can pay down your debt faster.

And if you have an opinion about forgiving $1.5 trillion in student loan debt or other policies aimed at helping borrowers, track legislation related to higher education and contact your representatives to let them know what you think.

5

Employers Could Help Pay Off Student Loans to Attract Top Talent

Arlene S. Hirsch

Arlene S. Hirsch is a career counselor and author. She is an expert in the field of career psychology.

With the unemployment rate at historic lows, companies often find that they have to offer a wide array of benefits and incentives to attract top talent. In the following viewpoint Arlene S. Hirsch explores the idea of companies paying off the student debt of their employees and looks into several variations on how such a plan might work. No one plan will work for all, but such solutions might very well be the way of the future.

The competition to attract and retain talent is fierce. The unemployment rate is at a near-historic low, and companies are offering sign-on bonuses, flexible hours and a range of other perks to fill even entry-level jobs. Yet one benefit that job hunters and young employees say they want isn't being embraced: employer repayment of student loan debt.

In the US, more than 44 million people collectively owe $1.5 trillion in student loans, according to the Federal Reserve. About 65 percent of that debt belongs to people under age 40. Seven out of 10 new college graduates, on average, owe $37,172.

"Employers Explore Repaying Student Loan Debt," by Arlene S. Hirsch, Society for Human Resource Management (SHRM), July 30, 2018. Reprinted by permission.

But this isn't strictly a Millennial issue. The Federal Reserve reports that 6.8 million student loan borrowers between ages 40 and 49 owe $33,765 each, on average. And the problem is likely to grow. The Congressional Budget Office estimates that $1.27 trillion in new federal student loans will be added between 2018 and 2028.

"One of the reasons that employers are taking notice is that student loan debt has a real impact on recruitment, retention and overall employee productivity," said Sangeeta Moorjani, head of workplace products for Fidelity Investments, a Boston-based financial services company. "In the war for talent, solutions to address student debt can give employers a competitive advantage."

Millennials Take the Reins

Millennials will make up 75 percent of the US labor force by 2025. That gives them a lot of negotiating power, and they're telling employers they need help with their student loans.

"Young workers feel highly stressed as a result of the burden of student debt, and that debt clearly impacts their health and productivity in the workplace," said Kevin Fudge, director of consumer advocacy at American Student Assistance (ASA), a nonprofit organization that helps eliminate financial barriers to education. "Employers should realize that in order to retain the brightest young talent and demonstrate their commitment to employee well-being, they need to provide concrete and straightforward solutions to help alleviate the burden of student loan debt."

An ASA survey of 500 employees ages 22 to 33 highlights how student loan debt negatively impacts their focus, well-being and retirement planning and delays their pursuit of additional education. More than half of the workers surveyed say they worry about student loan debt most or all of the time. Nearly 65 percent say they may seek a second job to help pay off their loans.

"When employees are distracted, they aren't being productive," said Peter Marcia, founder and CEO of YouDecide, a voluntary benefits outsourcing company in Atlanta.

The ASA findings read like a blueprint for companies that are seeking student-debt solutions:

- 86 percent of employees would commit to a company for five years if the employer helped pay back their student loans.
- 92 percent would take advantage of a match for student loan repayments similar to a 401(k) match.
- 89 percent would use long-term financial planning tools or advice.
- 79 percent would take advantage of free access to a student loan debt counselor.

Benefits experts agree that financial benefits programs are most successful when an organization identifies the unique concerns of its workforce and tailors the content to its employees. Yet 75 percent of the 450 HR professionals who participated in the ASA survey reported that their company doesn't address student loan debt. And the Society for Human Resource Management's (SHRM's) 2018 Employee Benefits survey found that only 4 percent of US companies offer this benefit. WorldatWork, an association of total rewards professionals, conducted a January 2017 benefits survey and also found that 4 percent of employers overall provided loan repayment assistance, while 8 percent of companies with 40,000 or more employees did so.

Student Loan Repayment Plans

One approach that is gaining interest among employers is student loan repayment plans (SLRPs). This benefit, which is usually administered through third-party vendors, allows employers to make monthly contributions directly to an employee's student loan servicer while employees continue to make regular payments. The monthly contribution, which is applied directly to the principal, can shave several years off each loan.

Early adopters tout SLRPs as an effective way to differentiate themselves from their competitors as an employer of choice.

"We expect it to help us recruit and retain good workers," said Mike Fenlon, chief people officer for PricewaterhouseCoopers (PwC), a global accounting and consulting firm. "It strengthens our brand."

PwC launched its Student Loan Paydown program in 2016. Forty-five percent of the firm's 46,000 junior employees (with six years' experience or less) signed up to receive up to $1,200 annually for six years. The firm has found that this program has become a contributing factor in the job acceptance rate among applicants.

At OCC, a Chicago-based equity derivatives clearinghouse, student loan assistance is the No. 1 benefit being talked about at job and recruiting fairs, said Erin Smith, first vice president of total rewards. "Most companies provide a pretty standard benefit menu, so when you introduce a program that differentiates you, that really matters," she said.

Aetna offers a repayment benefit that targets employees who obtained undergraduate or graduate degrees within three years of applying. Staples offers its SLRP to sales associates and high performers. Peloton, a high-tech fitness company based in New York City, offers its SLRP to any employee with undergraduate or graduate-school loans, regardless of whether he or she obtained a degree.

"The decision was a complete no-brainer for us," said Amy Stoldt, vice president of people for Peloton. "We anticipate it will help us broaden our recruiting pool, as well as retain top talent in our workforce."

SLRPs can also help with diversity initiatives, since women and minorities have disproportionately more student loan debt. A 2015 study conducted by EdAssist, a strategic tuition-assistance company, found that Millennial women were 50 percent more likely to have student loan debt than men, and more than 50 percent of applicants are likely to be attracted to an employer offering to help them repay their student loans.

To be sure, offering a SLRP can be expensive. Peter Marcia said that many employers are reluctant to budget for a new and potentially costly benefit, even if candidates are eager for the offering. Although legislation to make the benefit tax deductible is pending in Congress, SLRPs are currently treated as taxable income.

"When the benefit receives tax-favored status, more companies will start making contributions," predicted Katie Berliner, an account executive with YouDecide. "Our goal is to help clients take baby steps toward helping employees solve this problem."

Alternative Solutions

Since student loan benefits are still new, there's a lot of misinformation in the market, say benefits advisors. Many companies say that because the student loan process can be complicated and expensive, student loan benefit programs will be equally complicated and expensive.

In fact, expense is a big reason why adoption has been limited primarily to large corporations and small, tech-focused start-ups that must attract highly skilled Millennials. Another big detriment is fairness: Paying thousands of dollars more annually to workers with loans and not to their colleagues who don't have unpaid loans strikes some compensation experts as difficult to justify. Unlike tuition assistance, the payments are not improving workers' skills.

These drawbacks help explain the low adoption rate for the loan repayment benefit, despite a massive marketing push from vendors selling platforms and advisory services to put it into place. Another reason for slow adoption may be a lack of financial acumen among both employees and their managers.

"The foundation of any student loan benefit should be counseling and management resources," said a spokesperson for IonTuition, a student loan management and refinancing company. "Borrowers lack information about their repayment options, so if you can offer them access to expert guidance, you achieve a lot for a surprisingly low-resource investment."

Berliner agrees: "Financial counseling is paramount." Many borrowers first took out student loans as teenagers without really understanding how difficult it would be to repay them. Without any credit history, they often ended up with higher interest rates. As adults, they may still lack sound financial decision-making skills or the financial acumen to manage their debt effectively.

Fidelity's holistic approach to addressing employee student loan debt includes an SLRP (that pays $2,000 per year with a $10,000 cap), and financial counseling and education for employees at all career and life stages. In the development of the program, Fidelity leaders often heard employees express regret that they wish they'd known more when they were in high school and making decisions about how to finance their college education.

In response, Fidelity Labs, an in-house product incubator, created an online education platform called the Student Debt Tool to help employees better understand their situation and their options. The tool includes a student loan refinancing platform to help consolidate loans to achieve lower lending rates. It also offers tools and advice to help employees save for future college costs for themselves and their children.

"Precollege planning is critical to help ensure families are prepared to make the best decision possible for their specific situation so they're not surprised by how it impacts their financial wellness later," Moorjani said.

6

Have We Considered Crowdfunding Education?

Davide Migali

Davide Migali's work can be found on Medium. He is Senior Manager at OpenText (formerly Recommind) and is an experienced eDiscovery project manager and qualified lawyer.

Should education be treated as a commodity, subject to market forces of supply and demand? Should the government step in to intervene? Should private investors fund college students with the promise of getting a return, that is "owning" them? Everyone agrees that crippling student debts are hindering opportunities for the next generation of the workforce, delaying contributions to the economy. As well, students riddled with debt are less likely to take risks on innovations and entrepreneurship. Crowdfunding could be the solution.

All debts look alike.

A borrows from B and then A must repay a certain amount of money to B within a specific time frame.

Every loan shares this same basic structure. But, to the human eye—and heart—some debts are different.

If you had to choose, would you rather repay a friend or a bank? Would it make any difference to you knowing that your repayments will benefit your community or a cause you believe in, instead of simply enriching a for-profit organisation?

I would argue that, although law and economics treat all debts equally, humans don't. In a world where capital is scarce, this insight has important implications for the struggling education market.

The central difficulty is this: How to maintain high-quality education AND make it affordable for everyone?

The solution could be left to the market. Then opposing forces of supply and demand would find an equilibrium point (in reality, several different points), leaving buyers limited to only what they could afford.

But in the case of education, even the most ardent liberals would agree that it cannot be treated purely as a commodity. The dispassionate laws of the market are frequently adjusted to take account of what we consider to be a basic human right.

This moral quandary presents serious issues for governments across the world. Confronted by an ever-growing public debt and consequent fiscal constraints, political leaders are facing a dilemma—do they lower the quality of education, shift some of the burden of cost on to taxpayers, or charge the students the full cost of high-quality education?

When government and institutions fail in the provision of critical public services, private capital and investors are often asked to step in. For a price.

I have very little sympathy with government intervention in the market and I have always supported—and always will do—any opening for private investment. But with these critical public services, the government cannot simply abdicate its responsibility in favour of the private sector. A purely laissez faire attitude will not achieve an acceptable level of education for all.

Let's think about the United States, where a large industry has grown up around student loans.

With an overall debt of $1.2 trillion (a little more than $35,000 per student in 2015), and the steady decrease of public subsidies, the burden on the US students' shoulders will likely shape their lives forever. And thus the welfare of the entire country.

Decisions made in debt tend to be deeply conservative. An indebted student will be, for example, less inclined to become an entrepreneur, opting instead for a job with a steady pay check. Moreover, an educational system based on debt will increase social inequality, depriving the poor of the most reliable "social lift" ever invented.

A deeply unequal society where innovation is hindered is not how any country—the United States in particular—wants to be labelled. This is why it's already been such a feature of the 2016 Presidential campaign.

Hilary Clinton—as reported by *The Economist*—"proposes capping the repayment of college loans at a maximum of 10% of income over 20 years. If a loan is not paid off by then the government will pick up the tab". Good, but the collateral provided by the State offers no incentive for change for either lenders or students.

Marco Rubio, continues *The Economist*, wants to tackle the issue in a more aggressive way: "Under Mr Rubio's plan, private investors would pay for a student's education in return for a claim on a chunk of his future earnings. Just as dividends accruing to a shareholder depend on a firm's profits, so a student's subsequent payments to the investor would rise and fall with his income. Equity financing would lead to more informed choices because investors would be less willing to fund courses and colleges that offer low returns. And it would squeeze costs because unpopular courses would have to trim their spending".

This suggestion should be cheerfully welcomed and I do hope that this option will be offered to both students and investors. But, in spite of being a solid improvement, it is not the panacea a broken educational system needs, for at least a couple of reasons.

1. It might not be a good investment: While the idea may seem to benefit both parties, it might actually prove financially unsound. We all know that certain industries offer better

starting salaries and career progressions than others. Students know this too and therefore a student that is looking to enter a high paying profession, such as finance, will calculate that they are better off funding their studies using debt leverage instead of equity.

The same reasoning applies to all the industries with high potential ROE (return on equity), leaving investors deprived of the essential incomes of higher yield students. Without these incomes they could still achieve a decent return, especially if the risk is spread over individuals that belong to categories whose skills are in need and are likely to receive a steady, if not high, income. But because of the low ROE investors might be driven towards different markets, leaving the education system unfunded.

2. The evolutionary argument: Diversity fosters progress and, more importantly, it prevents extinction. Equity investors TODAY will decide to fund what they think will provide a high return in a distant TOMORROW. The effect would be a concentration of investments (and students) in certain fields, leaving others unfunded. It is impossible to determine if, in the future, we will still need lots of people in finance and law. Perhaps instead we'll need more historians or designers. Without foreknowledge, the best strategy is to ensure a high level of diversity in fields of study.

A Third Way

The educational system appears to be too complex for a "one size fits all" model. Debt and equity should co-exist and leave room for a third option.

While writing my master thesis on the abuse of economic dependence among enterprises, I asked the following question to an economics professor:

"If an entrepreneur knows that his supplier will face X transactional costs to exit the contract, then surely he can renegotiate the terms of the contract to his benefit. Even though it's unfair, it is still in the best interest of the supplier to accept the new terms as long as he can make a profit. Would you agree?"

The Professor: "I would agree from an economic point of view. But please do not forget that an entrepreneur, like any human being, has dignity."

This reply left its mark on me. Economics is more than math or money. There are values in an economy like trust, meaning and dignity. These cannot be counted, but they count.

As I said at the beginning of this article, the moral obligation of repaying a friend or a community is often stronger than the one which legally binds a debtor and his creditor. And the psychological effects of not repaying some debts can be harsher than any legal consequences.

This third way leverages the humanity of both creditors and debtors to create a self-sustaining, long term solution to student debt. The idea works as follows:

- Individuals donate (not lend) money to entity A (a non-profit)
- Entity A gives money to student B acquiring equity over his future earnings for a certain period of time
- Students B repays Entity A
- Entity A uses the money from Student B (plus the donations, plus the repayments received by other students) to fund Students C, D, E … under the same conditions

This is not a money-spinning idea. Any sum—minus administration costs—will be used to fund as many students as possible, while taking into account that some will never be able to afford full repayment. Yet, this lack of profit is actually the secret to its success.

This enterprise is not about making money. Instead it relies on the altruism which funds charities and NGOs in America alone to the tune of $358.38 billion dollars last year. It allows those with resources to make a real impact and change lives. And education is particularly life-changing.

While scholarships already exist, there are too few to allow everyone the education they deserve. Crowdfunding education can turn each of us [into] a modern Andrew Carnegie.

Reading this you may still have a couple of questions:

What if a student can but doesn't repay?

Then we sue him and get the money back. The contract is legally binding. Stealing money from a charity isn't good for criminal record or your karma.

Why equity and not debt?

A good point. In some ways debt could work equally well because a student will feel the moral obligation to repay his debt, thus reducing the amount of unpaid loans.

But there are some problems:

a. Students would still make decisions based on their indebtedness which as described before is neither good for the student nor society.

b. The charity would be forced to extend loans for specific courses with a high ROI because of the limited returns granted by interests on capital. This would limit the educational diversity so essential for a society to survive and thrive.

Equity, on the contrary, is certainly riskier but has unlimited upsides while facing limited losses. This type of business model is designed to benefit from uncertainty and, like Biotech or Software companies, is looking for positive Black Swans. Funding the education of the next Bill Gates could create almost limitless benefits for the charity and society.

I am also convinced of the transformative power of receiving a similar act of kindness.

Being chosen to be the recipient of someone else's generosity and knowing that you, in turn, will have the chance of giving the same opportunity to another person, will boost your performance and will push you to make the repayments in time.

Reciprocation is a formidable tool that has facilitated human relationships since the dawn of time. By simply re-framing a debt as an opportunity to give something back, the debtor role can be completely redefined.

I welcome comment—any kind—on the ideas above. For this to work, feedback is essential and we especially love some harsh criticism.

A special mention to my life-long friends Sandro and Renato Fillinich, with whom I share the paternity of this idea. They taught me that you do not have to be rich to change a life and this attempt is just the natural embodiment of this lesson.

7

Should We Just Make College Free?

Amelia Josephson

Amelia Josephson is a journalist covering financial literacy topics. Her areas of expertise include retirement and home buying. Her work has appeared in many outlets, including CBS News and The Simple Dollar.

While it might not solve the current problem of student debt, making college free for everyone would certainly stop it in the future. The idea is popular—and not just among people applying to college. Can the richest country in the world find the resources to offer free college for all? Or is it not a worthwhile investment for an uncertain future? In the following viewpoint, Amelia Josephson examines the pros and cons of free college for all, bringing up some points on both sides of the issue that aren't often discussed.

During the 2016 primary season we heard a lot about the issue of free college. Should every American be able to get a bachelor's degree at no cost? What are the pros and cons of free college? If you have student debt yourself or you have kids who plan to go to college, you probably have strong feelings one way or another.

2016 was a big year for the subject of free college. President Obama introduced a plan to make community college free, and presidential candidate Sen. Bernie Sanders wanted to make public

"The Pros and Cons of Free College," by Amelia Josephson, SmartAsset, May 18, 2018. Reprinted by permission.

university tuition free for all. Not sure what the arguments for and against free college are? We've got you covered.

Pro 1: Free College Would Expand Access to Education

Okay, this one is a little obvious, but offering free college tuition would make it possible for more people to pursue higher education. The bright young people who currently skip college because they can't afford it would have the opportunity to get a degree and get better jobs. The high cost of a degree would no longer be an obstacle. For many proponents of free college, it's a question of fairness. They say that access to a bachelor's degree should be accessible to everyone, especially because a B.A. or B.S. is increasingly necessary to get a good job.

Pro 2: A More Educated Population Would Have Economic and Social Benefits for the Country

If more Americans were living up to their potential, getting a college degree and getting better jobs, there would be positive ripple effects. Proponents of free college argue that the change would boost the country's productivity and GDP as people sorted themselves into more suitable, higher-paying jobs. There are also social benefits to having a more educated populace and helping young people find their path.

Pro 3: Students Would Be Free to Follow Their Passions and Abilities

Because the current college education system leaves many students with high amounts of debt, students' choices are constrained. They may choose a major they don't really love simply because it promises a higher future salary. They might go to a college that's not the best one they could get in to because it's cheaper. They might take fewer risks later in life because of their debt. High levels of debt discourage people from starting businesses, moving to another city in search of better job opportunities or changing jobs. If you eliminate student loan debt you eliminate these problems, with benefits for students and for the overall economy.

Pro 4: Free College Would Help Repair Historic Inequities

In the US, we don't just have a problem of people being too poor to pay for college. We have a problem of generations of inequity based on discrimination. If your great-grandparents, grandparents and parents all had the opportunity to go to college you're much more likely to have that opportunity yourself, both because of accumulated net worth across the generations and because going to college will be expected in your family. Many Americans don't have the opportunity to go to college because their parents and grandparents and so on didn't have the opportunity. Free college would help redress that inequity.

Con 1: The Rich Would Get Help They Don't Need

If we made college free for everyone we would be subsidizing the rich. Families that have the money to pay for some or all of the cost of a college education might choose instead to take advantage of free college at a public institution. In effect, the government—and taxpayers—would be subsidizing the rich. Critics of free college who point to this drawback often argue that a more targeted reform subsidizing college for the poor and the middle class would make more sense. They also point to the example of Brazil, a country with free college where wealthy students reap a lot of the benefits of tuition-free education at public universities.

Con 2: Free College Would Be Expensive

Some critics of free college say it would be too expensive to implement. If the idea of raising taxes is a no-go with you you're probably not a big fan of the free college idea. Some plans, such as the one Sen. Sanders proposed, would use a combination of federal and state funds to make public colleges tuition free. But many states have been slashing their higher education budgets, so some critics question how the money would be raised to pay for free college.

Con 3: It Could Flood the Market and Lead to Credential Creep

Some critics of the free college idea argue that it would lead to a flood of graduates with mediocre credentials all competing for a limited number of jobs. Then, these critics argue, committed workers would have to pursue some kind of graduate degree to stand out from the crowd. This would cost money, as well as leading to credential creep.

Con 4: It Offers No Way to Control What People Study

Some opponents of free college argue that the government shouldn't be subsidizing people's degrees in majors that aren't likely to lead to a good job. They might be okay with subsidizing STEM degrees but not, say, theater degrees. These critics would prefer a more targeted program that would give students fewer choices.

Bottom Line

If you're one of the millions of Americans struggling with student debt you might be sympathetic to the cause of free college tuition. If you're skeptical of "big government" you're probably not sold on the need for a big reform like free college tuition for all. Regardless of where you stand on the issue, it's helpful to understand the arguments in favor of free college and the points used against the proposal.

8

Government Subsidized College Is Not a Good Idea

Jarrett Skorup

Jarrett Skorup is the director of marketing and communications at the Mackinac Center for Public Policy. His work has been featured in The Wall Street Journal, *Fox News, and National Public Radio.*

In the following viewpoint, Jarrett Skorup dispenses with the benefits of government-subsidized college, instead focusing on the detriments. He proposes that the economic benefits of such a policy would not be all that supporters have claimed and that government-subsidized higher education would only increase the cost of college in the long run. He closes this viewpoint by pointing out that sending people to college does not necessarily mean those people will learn, nor that a college education will help them contribute to society.

When the government is in the business of handing out money, interest groups lobby to get it—or advocate to receive more than they are already getting.

So it is with spending on higher education.

As the Michigan Legislature debates the state budget for the upcoming fiscal year, more money for preschool, college and everything in between is being proposed. Over the long-term, the funding for those areas has increased dramatically. Taxpayers

"Five Reasons the Government Shouldn't Subsidize Higher Education," by Jarrett Skorup, Mackinac Center for Public Policy, February 13, 2013.

should be skeptical of the current reasons for subsidizing universities further.

Requests for more higher education funding is reported willingly in the media: It's the "most important investment" people can make. It sees "$17 in economic benefits" per dollar invested by the state. It results in "lifetime earning power."

But the central arguments are dubious for five main reasons:

1. There Is No Link Between Higher Education Subsidies and Economic Growth, and None Between College Degrees and Job Creation

Since 1980, Michigan has spent a much higher proportion of personal income on state government support for higher education than nearby states like Illinois and Ohio. According to Ohio University economist Richard Vedder, by the year 2000, the Mitten State was spending the sixth most in the country (2.34 percent of its personal income), double what Illinois was spending and much more than Ohio. This did not lead to higher growth as Michigan's economy performed among the worst in the country during that time period.

And states with a higher proportion of college graduates do not necessarily grow by adding more college degrees. A comparison of the number of state residents with a college degree with per capital income growth from 2000–2008 yields no correlation.

2. More Subsidies Equals More Waste

The number of administrators and service staff at Michigan's 15 public universities increased at a faster rate than full-time equivalent students. Administrators and service staff numbers went from 19,576 in 2005 to 22,472 in 2009, while full-time equivalent students increased from 250,030 to 257,230 over the same time period. At the same time, the compensation for the average employee increased 13 percent.

Michigan is not alone: A 2009 report from the Center for College Affordability and Productivity showed a 20-year increase in administration and support staff. And revenue for Michigan's public universities went from $4.2 billion to $5.0 billion, largely from higher tuition and fees. The average compensation for University of Michigan full-time faculty increased from $122,943 in 2005–06 to $141,753 in 2009–10. The University of Michigan–Flint now has more administrators than faculty.

Colleges set tuition rates relative to supply-and-demand, but government subsidies distort this process and inflate the cost. That's why schools like Grove City College (my alma mater) and Hillsdale College, which receive no government funding, do a much better job at keeping down the cost of tuition. Annual tuition at Grove City is $13,598, the cheapest of all institutions of higher education in Pennsylvania. Tuition at Hillsdale is $20,760 a year. Both are much cheaper than the average cost of private colleges and universities in the country at $31,975 a year.

3. When Comparing Earning Power Between College Graduates and Non-Graduates, Correlation Is Not Causation, and the Actual Cost of College Matters

Proponents of more funding for higher education almost always cite the same statistic as their main point: Overall, college graduates tend to make more money in their lifetime than those without a degree.

But this assumes that the degree caused the higher earnings, rather than the fact that those who complete college are already more likely to be financially successful whether they attend university or not.

The common figure cited is that a college degree is worth $1 million over the lifetime of a worker. Besides ignoring the point above, this is a poor exercise in statistics. The number is arrived at by taking the difference between the average pay of a college graduate and the average pay of a non-college graduate and multiplying it over a 40-year career.

First, that only tells us what the average is today, not what the actual future earnings are.

Second, this assumes that all college degrees have the same value. For example, it assumes that a Bachelor of Arts in art history is the same as a Bachelor of Science in quantum physics. Most significantly, it ignores many important factors: taxes, the real salary data of today's graduates, the opportunity cost of going to college (how much someone would earn during those years in school), the fact that a large proportion of students start school and do not finish, and, most importantly, student loan debt.

4. Ensuring That Everyone Has College Schooling Would Not Enhance the Labor Market—It Would Dilute a University Degree

The assumption among many is that every career should require a college education. This belief leads to subsidies for subjects with little practicality in the workforce and areas where a student may be better off doing an apprenticeship or working for four years than attending more school. Pushing for everyone to go to college does not automatically make those students university-ready, it lowers the overall standards of higher education. This has led to a high dropout rate, more repeated classes for those in school and an explosion of marginal subjects in which many degree-holders are forced to work outside that field because of a lack of demand. In short, incentivizing degrees students do not ever use.

5. Higher Education May Be the Next Bubble to Burst

Much like the housing bubble, higher education is fueled by government subsidies, publicly-backed loans and incentives that say everyone should be doing something. As noted and expanded on by law professor Glenn Reynolds, economist Richard Vedder and writer Nathan Harden, tuition costs have skyrocketed well above inflation while colleges compete to expand into areas outside of their main purpose and taking on more debt to do so. At the same time, competition from other sectors, like online education, offer cheaper alternatives to the bread-and-butter of university academia.

It is important for citizens to be educated, both to learn a job and to better be able to respond to a changing marketplace. But there is a difference between education and schooling.

Spending more money to send people to get a specific number of degrees at a specific institution is different from education. Education comes in the form of apprenticeships, trade schools and time on the job learning.

And education is something you can't force on someone else. Just putting someone in college does make force them to learn anything. Education is a personal matter, and more subsidies will only influence a person's decision to learn or not to learn at the barest of margins.

Higher education can build new skills, enhance old ones and show prospective employers that students are able to put in the time to earn a degree. But the value of a degree varies—by the institution, the cost, the time and the subject.

From an individual's perspective, college may be worth the cost. But for a growing number, it's not. And state subsidies, where political incentives trump market realities, only exacerbate that problem.

The Lending Business Is Stacked Against Student Borrowers

Ellen Brown

Ellen Brown is an attorney, author, and founder of the Public Banking Institute. She is author of the best-selling book, Web of Debt *(Third Millenium Press, 2012).*

Previous viewpoints have focused mainly on the economic consequences of student debt and various attempts to solve the crisis. In the following viewpoint, Ellen Brown explores some of the causes and contributors to the crisis. The author explains how the student loan industry is "stacked against student borrowers," and rife with fraud. She suggests several approaches governments (both federal and state) could take to deal with the crisis, including the establishment of state-owned banks.

The lending business is heavily stacked against student borrowers. Bigger players can borrow for almost nothing, and if their investments don't work out, they can put their corporate shells through bankruptcy and walk away. Not so with students. Their loan rates are high and if they cannot pay, their debts are not normally dischargeable in bankruptcy. Rather, the debts compound and can dog them for life, compromising not only their own futures but the economy itself.

"Student Debt Slavery: Time to Level the Playing Field," by Ellen Brown, *CounterPunch*, January 5, 2018. Reprinted by permission.

"Students should not be asked to pay more on their debt than they can afford," said Donald Trump on the presidential campaign trail in October 2016. "And the debt should not be an albatross around their necks for the rest of their lives." But as Matt Taibbi points out in a December 15 article, a number of proposed federal changes will make it harder, not easier, for students to escape their debts, including wiping out some existing income-based repayment plans, harsher terms for graduate student loans, ending a program to cancel the debt of students defrauded by ripoff diploma mills, and strengthening "loan rehabilitation"—the recycling of defaulted loans into new, much larger loans on which the borrower usually winds up paying only interest and never touching the principal. The agents arranging these loans can get fat commissions of up to 16 percent, an example of the perverse incentives created in the lucrative student loan market. Servicers often profit more when borrowers default than when they pay smaller amounts over a longer time, so they have an incentive to encourage delinquencies, pushing students into default rather than rescheduling their loans. It has been estimated that the government spends $38 for every $1 it recovers from defaulted debt. The other $37 goes to the debt collectors.

The securitization of student debt has compounded these problems. Like mortgages, student loans have been pooled and packaged into new financial products that are sold as student loan asset-backed securities (SLABS). Although a 2010 bill largely eliminated private banks and lenders from the federal student loan business, the "student loan industrial complex" has created a $200 billion market that allows banks to cash in on student loans without issuing them. About 80 percent of SLABS are government-guaranteed. Banks can sell, trade or bet on these securities, just as they did with mortgage-backed securities; and they create the same sort of twisted incentives for loan servicing that occurred with mortgages.

According to the Consumer Financial Protection Bureau (CFPB), virtually all borrowers with federal student loans are currently eligible to make monthly payments indexed to their earnings. That means there should be no defaults among student borrowers. Yet one in four borrowers is now in default or struggling to stay current. Why? Student borrowers are reporting widespread mishandling of accounts, unexplained exorbitant fees, and outright deception as they are bullied into default, tactics similar to those that homeowners faced in the foreclosure crisis. The reports reveal a repeat of the abuses of the foreclosure fraud era: many borrowers are unable to obtain basic information about their accounts, are frequently misled, are surprised with unexpected late fees, and often are pushed into default. Servicers lose paperwork or misapply payments. When errors arise, borrowers find it difficult to have them corrected.

Abuses and fraud in handling student loans have brought the Education Department's loan contractors under fire. In January 2017, the Consumer Financial Protection Bureau sued Navient, one of the largest contractors, alleging that the company "systematically and illegally [failed] borrowers at every stage of [student loan] repayment."

Getting a Fair Deal

The federal government could relieve these debt burdens, given the political will. A stated goal of the changes being proposed by the Trump Administration is to simplify the rules. The simplest solution to the student debt crisis is to make tuition free for qualified applicants at public colleges and universities, as it is in many European countries and was in some US states until the 1970s. If the federal government has the money to lend to students, it has the money to spend on their tuition (capped to curb tuition hikes). It would not only save on defaults and collections but could turn a profit on the investment, as demonstrated by the seven-fold return from the G.I. Bill.

Alternatively, the government could fund tuition costs and debtor relief with a form of "QE for the people." Instead of buying mortgage-backed securities, as in QE1, the Fed could buy SLABS and return the interest to students, making the loans effectively interest-free (as were the $16+ trillion in loans made to the largest banks after the 2008 crisis). QE that targeted the real economy could address many other budget issues as well, including the infrastructure crisis and the federal debt crisis; and this could be done without triggering hyperinflation. See my earlier articles here, here and here.

Needless to say, however, the government is not moving in that direction. While waiting for the government to act, there are things students can do; but first they need to learn their rights. According to a new survey reported in November 2017, students are often in the dark about key details of their student loan debt and the repayment options available to them. To get started, see here and here.

Under the Borrower's Defense to Repayment program, you can get your loans completely discharged if you can prove they were based on deception or fraud. That is one of the alternatives the Administration wants to take away, so haste is advised; but even if it is taken away, fraud remains legal grounds for contract rescission. A class action for treble damages against offending institutions could provide significant financial relief.

Students also have greater bankruptcy options than they know. While current bankruptcy law exempts education loans and obligations from eligibility for discharge, an exception is made for "undue hardship." The test normally used is that paying the loan will prevent the borrower from sustaining a minimum standard of living, his financial situation is unlikely to change in the future, and he has made a good faith effort to pay his loans. According to a 2011 study, at least 40 percent of borrowers who included their student loans in their bankruptcy filings got some or all of their student debt discharged. But because they think there is no chance, they rarely try. Only about 0.1 percent of consumers with student loans attempted to include them in their bankruptcy proceedings. (Getting a knowledgeable attorney is advised.)

For relief as a class, students need to get the attention of legislators, which means getting organized. Along with degree mill fraud and contract fraud, a cause of action ripe for a class action is the student exclusion from bankruptcy protection, a blatant violation of the "equal protection" clause of the Fourteenth Amendment. If enough students filed for bankruptcy under the "undue hardship" exception, just the administrative burden might motivate legislators to change the law.

States to the Rescue?

If the federal government won't act and individual action seems too daunting, however, there is a third possibility for relief—state-owned banks that cut out private middlemen and recycle local money for local purposes at substantially reduced rates. The country's sole model at the moment is the Bank of North Dakota, but other states now have strong public banking movements that could mimic it. A November 2014 article in the *Wall Street Journal* reported that the BND was more profitable even than J.P. Morgan Chase and Goldman Sachs. The profits are used to improve education and public services.

According to its 2016 annual report, the BND's second largest loan category after business loans is for education, with nearly a third of its portfolio going to student loans. As of December 2017, the BND's student loan rates were 2.82% variable and 4.78% fixed, or about 2% below the federal rate (which ranged from 4.45% to 7% depending on the type of loan), and about 5% below the private rate (currently averaging 9.66% fixed and 7.81% variable interest). The BND also acts as the servicer of these loans, bypassing the third-party servicers abusing the system in other states.

In 2014, the BND launched its DEAL One Loan program, which offered North Dakota residents a unique option to refinance all student loans, including federal, into one loan with a lower interest rate and without fees. DEAL loans are fully guaranteed by the North Dakota Guaranteed Student Loan Program, which is administered by the BND.

The BND also makes 20-year school construction loans available at a very modest 2% interest. Compare that to the Capital Appreciation Bonds through which many California schools have been forced to borrow to build needed infrastructure, on which they have wound up owing as much as 15 times principal.

The BND's loan programs have helped keep North Dakota's student default rates and overall student indebtedness low. As of January 2017, the state had the second lowest student default rate in the country and was near the bottom of the list in student indebtedness, ranking 44th. Compare that to its sister state South Dakota, which ranked number one in student indebtedness.

The public banking movement is now gaining ground in cities and states across the country. A number of cities have passed resolutions to pull their money out of Wall Street banks that practice fraud as a business model. In New Jersey, Governor-elect Phil Murphy has made a state-owned bank the funding basis of his platform, with student loans one of three sectors he intends to focus on. If that succeeds, other states can be expected to follow suit.

We need to free our students from the system of debt slavery that has financialized education, turning it from an investment in human capital into a tool for exploiting the young for the benefit of private investors. State-owned banks can make the loan process fair, equitable and affordable; but their creation will be fought by big bank lobbyists. An organized student movement could be an effective counter-lobby. Historically, debt and austerity have been used as control mechanisms for subduing the people. It is time for the people to unite and take back their power.

10

We Should Return to the Idea of Education as a Public Good

Thomas Adam

Thomas Adam is an expert in Transnational History, Global History, Philanthropy and Civil Society Studies, and German history. He has been a professor of transnational history at the University of Texas at Arlington since 2001.

In the following viewpoint Thomas Adam examines the historical roots of college tuition. The cost of college, he explains, changed as people's ideas about the purpose of college changed. When higher education was considered a pubic good—that people who received a college education would put that education to work improving society—tuition was free. Only when college came to be seen as a "vehicle for individual enrichment," did the practice of charging students for college take hold. The solution, he argues, is to return to the notion of college as a public good.

The promise of free college education helped propel Bernie Sanders' 2016 bid for the Democratic nomination to national prominence. It reverberated during the confirmation hearings for Betsy DeVos as Secretary of Education and Sanders continues to push the issue.

In conversations among politicians, college administrators, educators, parents and students, college affordability seems to be seen as a purely financial issue—it's all about money.

My research into the historical cost of college shows that the roots of the current student debt crisis are neither economic nor financial in origin, but predominantly social. Tuition fees and student loans became an essential part of the equation only as Americans came to believe in an entirely different purpose for higher education.

Cost of a College Degree Today

For many students, graduation means debt. In 2012, more than 44 million Americans (14 percent of the total population) were still paying off student loans. And the average graduate in 2016 left college with more than $37,000 in student loan debt.

Student loan debt has become the second-largest type of personal debt among Americans. Besides leading to depression and anxiety, student loan debt slows down economic growth: It prevents young Americans from buying houses and cars and starting a family. Economist Alvaro Mezza, among others, has shown that there is a negative correlation between increasing student loan debt and homeownership.

The increase in student loan debt should come as no surprise given the increasing cost of college and the share that students are asked to shoulder. Decreasing state support for colleges over the last two decades caused colleges to raise tuition fees significantly. From 1995 to 2015, tuition and fees at 310 national universities ranked by US News rose considerably, increasing by nearly 180 percent at private schools and over 225 percent at public schools.

Whatever the reason, tuition has gone up. And students are paying that higher tuition with student loans. These loans can influence students' decisions about which majors to pick and whether to pursue graduate studies.

Early Higher Education: A Public Good

During the 19th century, college education in the United States was offered largely for free. Colleges trained students from middle-class backgrounds as high school teachers, ministers and community leaders who, after graduation, were to serve public needs.

This free tuition model had to do with perceptions about the role of higher education: College education was considered a public good. Students who received such an education would put it to use in the betterment of society. Everyone benefited when people chose to go to college. And because it was considered a public good, society was willing to pay for it—either by offering college education free of charge or by providing tuition scholarships to individual students.

Stanford University, which was founded on the premise of offering college education free of charge to California residents, was an example of the former. Stanford did not charge tuition for almost three decades from its opening in 1891 until 1920.

Other colleges, such as the College of William and Mary, offered comprehensive tuition scholarship programs, which covered tuition in exchange for a pledge of the student to engage in some kind of service after graduation. Beginning in 1888, William and Mary provided full tuition scholarships to about one third of its students. In exchange, students receiving this scholarship pledged to teach for two years at a Virginia public school.

And even though the cost for educating students rose significantly in the second half of the 19th century, college administrators such as Harvard President Charles W. Eliot insisted that these costs should not be passed on to students. In a letter to Charles Francis Adams dated June 9, 1904, Eliot wrote, "I want to have the College open equally to men with much money, little money, or no money, provided they all have brains."

College Education Becomes a Private Pursuit

The perception of higher education changed dramatically around 1910. Private colleges began to attract more students from upper-class families—students who went to college for the social experience and not necessarily for learning.

This social and cultural change led to a fundamental shift in the defined purpose of a college education. What was once a public good designed to advance the welfare of society was becoming a private pursuit for self-aggrandizement. Young people entering college were no longer seen as doing so for the betterment of society, but rather as pursuing personal goals: in particular, enjoying the social setting of private colleges and obtaining a respected professional position upon graduation.

In 1927, John D. Rockefeller began campaigning for charging students the full cost it took to educate them. Further, he suggested that students could shoulder such costs through student loans. Rockefeller and like-minded donors (in particular, William E. Harmon, the wealthy real estate magnate) were quite successful in their campaign. They convinced donors, educators and college administrators that students should pay for their own education because going to college was considered a deeply personal affair. Tuition—and student loans—thus became commonly accepted aspects of the economics of higher education.

The shift in attitude regarding college has also become commonly accepted. Altruistic notions about the advancement of society have generally been pushed aside in favor of the image of college as a vehicle for individual enrichment.

A New Social Contract

If the United States is looking for alternatives to what some would call a failing funding model for college affordability, the solution may lie in looking further back than the current system, which has been in place since the 1930s.

In the 19th century, communities and the state would foot the bill for college tuition because students were contributing to society. They served the common good by teaching high school for a certain number of years or by taking leadership positions within local communities. A few marginal programs with similar missions (ROTC and Teach for America) still exist today, but students participating in these programs are very much in the minority.

Instead, higher education today seems to be about what college can do for you. It's not about what college students can do for society.

I believe that tuition-free education can only be realized if college education is again reframed as a public good. For this, students, communities, donors and politicians would have to enter into a new social contract that exchanges tuition-free education for public services.

11

College Is Worth the Debt

Jana Kasperkevic

Jana Kasperkevic is a digital reporter for Marketplace. At the time of this writing, she was a business reporter at The Guardian *where she covered the global economy, income inequality, personal finance and small business. Her work has appeared in* Inc. *magazine,* Houston Chronicle, *and* The Village Voice, *among others.*

Particularly in a difficult job market, many people argue that a college education is no longer worth the cost—especially when it means a four-year delay entering the job market and years of indebtedness once you're there. Here, the author cites a study by the Federal Reserve Bank of New York that indicates college graduates do indeed make back their investment in the long run.

To all the college grads out there, sighing over their student loan payments, the Federal Reserve Bank of New York has a message: it was all worth it.

If you regret spending all that money on a college education, you are not alone. About 31% of millennials regret paying for college instead of trying to get a job out of high school, according to Wells Fargo.

Yet thanks to that expensive education, over the course of their lives college graduates are bound to recoup all the money

"College Education Is Worth the Debt of Admission, Says New York Fed Study," by Jana Kasperkevic, Guardian News and Media Ltd, June 24, 2014. Reprinted by permission.

they spent getting their degree—and much more, says the New York Fed.

"Over the past four decades, those with [a] bachelor's degree have tended to earn 56% more than high school graduates while those with an associate's degree have tended to earn 21% more than high school graduates," found the report.

In their lifetime, college graduates are likely to earn about $1m more, the Fed said. Those with an associate degree earn about $325,000 more in their lifetime than high school graduates.

There is a caveat here: the real cost of college education, according to the New York Fed, is the net cost of tuition and the opportunity cost of lost wages—meaning the money students give up by not working full-time during their college years.

And while these numbers sound great in the long term, leaving college to search for work in the current market is not easy, and requires resilience and patience.

Especially if, like most US students, you graduate with about $30,000 in loans.

Strangely, student loan debt, which amounts to about $1tn in the US, is something the New York Fed report authors chose not to incorporate into their analysis on the rate of return of an education.

There are a few other factors in the cost of an education that the authors omitted.

Not only did the report not incorporate student debt, but the tuition estimates used in the analysis are the net tuition costs, which don't include room and board.

The report estimates the total cost of four-year tuition to be $26,000, arguing that the net price of a bachelor's degree is $6,550 a year—well below the annual $14,750 sticker price. At many private colleges, particularly elite ones such as those in the Ivy League, the sticker price is above $50,000.

And the cost of the associate degree, according to the Fed? $0. In fact, less than zero. "[T]he actual cost of an associate's degree was more than fully subsidized by various tax benefits and other form of aid," noted the report.

Opportunity Cost

The opportunity cost of going to college—missing out on two or four years of full-time wages—is not that high, found the New York Fed.

The wages that American students miss out on, should they not enter the labor market after high school, totals $96,000 for those pursuing a four-year bachelor's degree, and $46,000 for those pursuing an associate degree. College graduates are likely to make up for those lost wages within a few years, thanks to the higher pay ensured by their degrees.

What About the Debt?

Despite the fact that everyone, from President Obama to Starbucks CEO Howard Schultz, is worried about the student debt crisis that plagues US college graduates, the New York Fed believes that student loans are cheap subsidies.

The authors write:

> In exchange for paying interest, people can take out student loans to delay paying their college expenses. Thus, it is not necessary to incorporate such financing options into our rate of return analysis. In face, because interest rates on student loans are often subsidized at below-market rates, student loans generally allow people to earn higher returns than our results would indicate.

While it's true that federal loans are often subsidized at below-market rates and hover at less than 6% interest rates, not all students are eligible for such loans.

As a result, a number of students rely on private loans, which come with interest rates as high as 18%. As of 2012, there were $150bn in private student loans. Even if the New York Fed didn't deem these loans and interest rates important enough to consider when evaluating the worth of one's education, the students who took out those loans are keenly aware of their costs.

A newly released study by the Brookings Institution came to the conclusion that US households with extreme student debt burdens are not the norm, but are "exceptional cases".

Working off of Federal Reserve Bank's Survey of Consumer Finance, the report found that 58% of those households have less than $10,000 in debt and 18% have debt between $10,000 to $20,000.

The problem is that this assessment looks at all households with student debt, including those who have been paying off their burden for years.

Therefore, the debt analyzed in the study is not the original debt taken out, but what remains after years of payments.

Buried in the Brookings study is the one thing that really matters to recent graduates and to younger Americans still debating whether college is worth it: the fact that, on average, "bachelor's degree recipients in 2011-12 who took out student loans accumulated an average debt load of approximately $26,000 ($25,000 at public institutions, and $29,900 at private, nonprofit institutions)."

That means that new generation of college graduates are dealing with much greater burden of debt than those who came before them.

A Degree Is No Longer the Quickest, Surest Way to a Well-Paid Job

It has been the burden of student loan debt, in fact, that has caused college graduates to question the point of a college degree. The current unemployment rate for college graduates might be 3.2% but that still translates into more than 1.5m unemployed Americans who have bachelor's degree or higher. When so many people have a college degree, it is no longer a guarantee that one will get a job.

Then there are those students who found jobs where their college degree hasn't improved their prospects. The current underemployment rate for recent college graduates is 18.8%.

And while employment prospects get better with time, it does not apply to everyone, admits the report.

[T]he likelihood of being underemployed declines significantly with age, and more college graduates work their way into college-level

jobs by the time they reach their thirties. Nonetheless, about a third of those who obtain a college degree do spend much of their careers in jobs that typically do not require a bachelor's degree.

Interestingly, the report found that even though college graduates are increasingly working jobs that do not require a high of a level of education, they are still getting something out of their degree.

"Employers are willing to pay a premium for college graduates relative to those with just a high school diploma, even in jobs that are not typically considered college-level positions," notes the report.

According to the Economic Policy Institute, the average wage for college graduates is $16.60, as compared to just $9.48 for high school graduates. So while college graduates might not be working the jobs they imagined they would be based on their level of education, they are still making more than those who did not attend college.

Degrees as Stocks

In order to drive home the point of why higher education is still worth time and money, the report's authors presented degrees as stocks, pointing out that they actually have a great rate of return.

"To put these findings in perspective, consider that investing in stocks has yielded an annual return of 7% and investing in bonds an annual return of 3% since 1950," notes the report. "A return of at least 7% is clearly a good investment because it exceeds the historical return on stocks; a return below 3% would be a poor investment since one could do better by investing in bonds."

The return on a bachelor degree, which averaged about 9% during the 1970s, reached peak return of about 16% in 2001. It has since remained within the 14% to 15% range. Similarly, the return for associates degree ranges between 13% to 15%.

Yet just like stocks, not all degrees are created equal. Some will perform better than others.

For example, technical training degrees are likely to have a higher rate of return. The report found that engineering majors and math and computer majors had rates of return 21% and 18%, respectively.

On the other end of the spectrum are degrees in majors like liberal arts, hospitality and leisure, which the report says have "below-average returns." Even those low returns are still worth it, however, as "each major has a rate of return exceeding 9%."

Another report from the New York Fed, released in January of this year, found that the graduates with these under-performing degrees most often find themselves underemployed, working lower-paid jobs that sometimes don't even require a college degree.

As difficult as things might seem for college graduates, they could always be worse. Just think about those Americans who never went to college, says the New York Fed.

"Despite the recent struggles of college graduates, investing in a college degree may be more important than ever before because those who fail to do so are falling further and further behind."

12

The Effects of Student Borrowing on the Larger Economy Are Limited

Sandra Black, Amy Filipek, Jason Furman, Laura Giuliano and Ayushi Narayan

Sandra Black is Professor of Economics at the University of Texas Austin. Amy Filipek is a staff economist at the Council of Economic Advisors. Jason Furman is Professor of the Practice of Economic Policy at Harvard University. Laura Giuliano is a senior economist with the Council of Economic Advisors and Associate Professor of Economics at the University of Miami. Ayushi Narayan is a research economist with the Council of Economic Advisors.

In the following viewpoint, written in August 2016 near the end of the Obama administration, Sandra Black, Amy Filipek, Jason Furman, Laura Giuliano and Ayushi Narayan consider the student debt problem from the point of view of the larger economy, not just the student borrowers. The authors say that while the return on investment can vary for individuals, the effects of overall student debt on the larger economy are limited and that many of the government policies at that time (many have since been scaled back) were helping mitigate the problem.

S tudent debt has increased rapidly in the US over the past 20 years and currently totals over $1.3 trillion. A rising number of students are taking out loans, and today, roughly half of students

"Student Loans and College Quality: Effects on Borrowers and the Economy," by Sandra Black, Amy Filipek, Jason Furman, Laura Giuliano and Ayushi Narayan, VoxEU.org, August 4, 2016. Reprinted by permission.

borrow to pay for the tuition and living expenses associated with a college education. This trend has led some to question whether we are facing a student debt "crisis," and a growing body of research has assessed the validity of this claim (e.g. Avery and Turner 2012, Looney and Yannelis 2015). A new report by the Council of Economic Advisers (2016) offers a comprehensive perspective on the economic benefits and challenges of student loans. Drawing on current research and new data from the Department of Education, it shows that on average, student loans facilitate very high returns for college graduates in the form of a high earnings premium, and most borrowers are able to make progress paying back their loans. But, borrowers who attend low quality schools or fail to complete their degree face real challenges with repayment. And even students whose lifetime return far exceeds their debt can have trouble with repayment at the start of their careers, when they are starting out and are not reaping the full earnings benefit of their additional education. Addressing these challenges has been a high priority of the Obama Administration, and policies to help students make better enrollment choices, better regulate for profit educational institutions, and make repayment more flexible, particularly through models allowing payments to vary with income, have begun to show results.

The Benefits of Higher Education Greatly Outweigh the Costs, on Average

The college earnings premium has grown steadily over the past several decades and reached historical levels in recent years. Compared to high school graduates, bachelor's degree recipients typically earn $500,000 more in present value over their lifetime—well above the roughly $30,000 of debt that borrowers accumulate on average for that degree. With such high returns, higher education is typically a strong investment, and most who borrow are able to repay their debt.

While part of the increase in total student debt is due to the increase in the number of students who enroll in college, there has also been an increase in the typical amount of debt that borrowers accumulate. One explanation for this is increasing college costs, in part due to a decline in state funding for public colleges. However, while published costs have risen sharply over the past couple of decades, a doubling of investments in Pell Grants and tax credits has helped to moderate the impact on the net price that students pay. Indeed, most students accumulate only modest amounts of debt: 59% of borrowers owe less than $20,000 in debt, with the undergraduate borrowers holding an average debt of $17,900 in 2015. Similarly, large-volume debt remains more prevalent among graduate loans.

All this suggests that, on average, the benefits of borrowing to invest in a college education continue to far exceed the costs.

But Many Students Still Face Debt Challenges, Especially Due to Variation in College Quality and Completion

While the earnings premium is typically very high, the returns students see after they leave school vary significantly. Students who fail to complete a degree or attend a low-quality institution that does not strengthen their labour market prospects can see lower returns (e.g. Hoekstra 2009, Cellini and Turner 2016) and face difficulty in repaying loans.

One important predictor of repayment difficulty is the failure to complete a degree. This relationship is so strong that it leads to a counterintuitive pattern in repayment outcomes: students with the smallest loan balances actually struggle the most with repayment. These students typically have lower balances because they have spent less time in school and are also the least likely to have completed a degree. In fact, the data show that loan size, for the most part, is positively related to the ability to repay. Large-volume debt is far more prevalent among graduate students, who have the higher earnings and thus a lower probability of default.

Similarly, among undergraduate borrowers, those with the largest debt size are more likely to have completed a degree, which decreases the probability of default regardless of debt size. Among those who complete a degree, undergraduate borrowers who graduated with less than $5,000 in debt have similar likelihoods of defaulting as those who graduated with larger amounts of debt. However, fewer than 1 in 6 undergraduate borrowers with only $5,000 of initial debt completed college, compared to nearly 2 in 3 borrowers with over $20,000 in debt.

Another related correlate of repayment is college sector. In particular, compared to students who attend community colleges or other non-selective schools, students at for-profits institutions tend to have lower earnings but hold larger amounts of debt (Deming et al. 2012, 2013). More rigorous research confirms that for-profit colleges offer lower returns than other sectors (Cellini and Turner 2016, Cellini and Chaudhary 2013). Consistent with this research, data from the Department of Education show that for-profit students face high rates of default—which is especially concerning in light of the high borrowing rate at these schools. Low-income borrowers and those who attend part-time are also more likely to default, in a pattern consistent with the type of schools they attend and their propensity to complete a degree.

While a Challenge for Some People, the Aggregate Macroeconomic Effects of Student Debt Are Limited

Additional college education, even if financed by student debt, is a big net positive for the economy—increasing skills, productivity, earnings and output. Conditional on a certain amount of college education, additional debt can be a small negative for the economy through reduced expenditures such as home purchases—although, to date, it has not had a large macroeconomic effect in part because as student debt has risen other debt has fallen.

The evidence is clear that the rise in student debt differs in important ways from the rise in mortgage debt. Although student debt has risen to be the second largest category of consumer debt, it continues to make up a small share of aggregate income. In 2015, total student loan debt was 9% of aggregate income, up from 3% in 2003. At its peak in 2007, total mortgage debt was 84% of aggregate income, up 25 percentage points in less than five years. Additionally, the private financial system is not exposed to student loan defaults in the way it was to subprime mortgages since the vast majority of student loans are explicitly guaranteed by the US government.

Some recent research has found that higher student loan balances—conditional on the same amount of education—can lower homeownership rates. However, these estimates can explain less than a quarter of the decline in homeownership among young households over the last decade and do not incorporate the positive impact of higher education levels. Research that takes into account the positive impact of college highlights that education levels drive home ownership more than debt levels. A study by Mezza et al. (2014) has shown that while early in life those with a college education and no student loan debt are more likely to be homeowners than those with debt, by age 34, their homeownership rates are nearly identical and more than 10 percentage points higher than for those without a college education.

The Obama Administration's Policies Are Also Helping

To help more students gain the economic benefits of higher education while minimising the risks of failing to complete a degree and receiving a low-quality education, the Obama Administration has implemented a number of evidence-based policies. To address information barriers about the return to individual colleges, the Administration has improved information about college cost and quality through the new College Scorecard, and it has protected students from low-quality schools through landmark regulations that will cut off federal aid to career college programmes consistently failing accountability standards. Recent improvements to the Free Application for Federal Student Aid (FAFSA) are helping to reduce procedural complexities that can prevent students from applying for aid. And increases in Pell Grants and tax aid have offset much of the rise in college tuitions.

Finally, the Administration has made significant progress toward making debt repayment more manageable by providing borrowers with more flexibility in their repayment options. Data show that the college earnings premium increases substantially over time. Yet the standard repayment plan requires fixed level payments over ten years—imposing constraints that may lead to needless repayment difficulties. The expansion of flexible income driven repayment plans such as the President's Pay as You Earn (PAYE) plan has lifted these constraints for millions of borrowers. These plans better align the timing of loan payments with the timing of earnings benefits by allowing borrowers to make smaller payments early in their careers and to adjust their payments as their earnings grow.

Today, about 5 million borrowers are enrolled in PAYE and other income driven repayment plans, representing a dramatic increase over the past four years. Data presented in CEA's report show that these plans disproportionately help borrowers from lower income families, and those who have struggled to repay their debt. Still, more work remains to increase enrollment in these plans by all those who could benefit from them.

References

Avery, C. and S. Turner (2012), "Student Loans: Do College Students Borrow Too Much—Or Not Enough?" *The Journal of Economic Perspectives* 26(1): 165-192.

Cellini, S. and L. Chaudhary (2013), "The Labor Market Returns to a For-Profit College Education." Working Paper.

Cellini, S. and N. Turner (2016), "Gainfully Employed? Assessing the Employment and Earnings of For-Profit College Students Using Administrative Data." NBER Working Paper No. 22287.

Council of Economic Advisers (2016), Investing in Higher Education: Benefits, Challenges, and the State of Student Debt.

Deming, D. J., C. Goldin, and L. F. Katz (2012), "The For-Profit Postsecondary School Sector: Nimble Critters or Agile Predators?" *Journal of Economic Perspectives* 276(1): 139-164.

Deming, D. J., C. Goldin, and L. F. Katz (2013), "For-Profit Colleges." *Future of Children* 23(1): 137-163.

Hoekstra, M. (2009), "The Effect of Attending the Flagship State University on Earnings: A Discontinuity-Based Approach." *The Review of Economics and Statistics* 91(4): 717-724.

Looney, A. and C. Yannelis (2015), "A Crisis in Student Loans? How Changes in the Characteristics of Borrowers and in the Institutions They Attended Contributed to Rising Loan Defaults." Brookings Papers on Economic Activity.

Mezza, A., K. Sommer, and S. Sherlund (2014), "Student Loans and Homeownership Trends." FEDS Notes October 15. Board of Governors of the Federal Reserve System.

13

Free College Would Reawaken the Concept of Education as a Public Good

Tressie McMillan Cottom

Tressie McMillan Cottom is an assistant professor of sociology at Virginia Commonwealth University and author of Lower Ed: The Troubling Rise of For-Profit Colleges in the New Economy *(The New Press, 2018).*

Throughout this volume, the idea of free college has come up again and again. In the following viewpoint Tressie McMillan Cottom frames the question of whether college should be free in a context greater than its economic effect. She discusses the cultural and sociological reasons for college attendance and why free college would help only the already relatively privileged. The true value of free college, the author argues, is a return to the concept of education as a collective good.

Free college is not a new idea, but, with higher education costs (and student loan debt) dominating public perception, it's one that appeals to more and more people—including me. The national debate about free, public higher education is long overdue. But let's get a few things out of the way.

College is the domain of the relatively privileged, and will likely stay that way for the foreseeable future, even if tuition is eliminated. As of 2012, over half of the US population has "some college" or

"Why Free College Is Necessary," by Tressie McMillan Cottom, *Dissent Magazine*, March 2014. Reprinted by permission.

postsecondary education. That category includes everything from an auto-mechanics class at a for-profit college to a business degree from Harvard. Even with such a broadly conceived category, we are still talking about just half of all Americans.

Why aren't more people going to college? One obvious answer would be cost, especially the cost of tuition. But the problem isn't just that college is expensive. It is also that going to college is complicated. It takes cultural and social, not just economic, capital. It means navigating advanced courses, standardized tests, forms. It means figuring out implicit rules—rules that can change.

Eliminating tuition would probably do very little to untangle the sailor's knot of inequalities that make it hard for most Americans to go to college. It would not address the cultural and social barriers imposed by unequal K–12 schooling, which puts a select few students on the college pathway at the expense of millions of others. Neither would it address the changing social milieu of higher education, in which the majority are now non-traditional students. ("Non-traditional" students are classified in different ways depending on who is doing the defining, but the best way to understand the category is in contrast to our assumptions of a traditional college student—young, unfettered, and continuing to college straight from high school.) How and why they go to college can depend as much on things like whether a college is within driving distance or provides one-on-one admissions counseling as it does on the price.

Given all of these factors, free college would likely benefit only an outlying group of students who are currently shut out of higher education because of cost—students with the ability and/or some cultural capital but without wealth. In other words, any conversation about college is a pretty elite one even if the word "free" is right there in the descriptor.

The discussion about free college, outside of the Democratic primary race, has also largely been limited to community colleges, with some exceptions by state. Because I am primarily interested in education as an affirmative justice mechanism, I would like all minority-serving and historically black colleges (HBCUs)—almost all of which qualify as four-year degree institutions—to be included. HBCUs disproportionately serve students facing the intersecting effects of wealth inequality, systematic K–12 disparities, and discrimination. For those reasons, any effort to use higher education as a vehicle for greater equality must include support for HBCUs, allowing them to offer accessible degrees with less (or no) debt.

The Obama administration's free community college plan, expanded in July to include grants that would reduce tuition at HBCUs, is a step in the right direction. Yet this is only the beginning of an educational justice agenda. An educational justice policy must include institutions of higher education but cannot only include institutions of higher education. Educational justice says that schools can and do reproduce inequalities as much as they ameliorate them. Educational justice says one hundred new Universities of Phoenix is not the same as access to high-quality instruction for the maximum number of willing students. And educational justice says that jobs programs that hire for ability over "fit" must be linked to millions of new credentials, no matter what form they take or how much they cost to obtain. Without that, some free college plans could reinforce prestige divisions between different types of schools, leaving the most vulnerable students no better off in the economy than they were before.

Free college plans are also limited by the reality that not everyone wants to go to college. Some people want to work and do not want to go to college forever and ever—for good reason. While the "opportunity costs" of spending four to six years earning a degree instead of working used to be balanced out by the promise of a "good job" after college, that rationale no longer holds, especially for poor students. Free-ninety-nine will not change that.

I am clear about all of that … and yet I don't care. I do not care if free college won't solve inequality. As an isolated policy, I know that it won't. I don't care that it will likely only benefit the high achievers among the statistically unprivileged—those with above-average test scores, know-how, or financial means compared to their cohort. Despite these problems, today's debate about free college tuition does something extremely valuable. It reintroduces the concept of public good to higher education discourse—a concept that fifty years of individuation, efficiency fetishes, and a rightward drift in politics have nearly pummeled out of higher education altogether. We no longer have a way to talk about public education as a collective good because even we defenders have adopted the language of competition. President Obama justified his free community college plan on the grounds that "Every American ... should be able to earn the skills and education necessary to compete and win in the twenty-first century economy." Meanwhile, for-profit boosters claim that their institutions allow "greater access" to college for the public. But access to what kind of education? Those of us who believe in viable, affordable higher ed need a different kind of language. You cannot organize for what you cannot name.

Already, the debate about if college should be free has forced us all to consider what higher education is for. We're dusting off old words like class and race and labor. We are even casting about for new words like "precariat" and "generation debt." The Debt Collective is a prime example of this. The group of hundreds of students and graduates of (mostly) for-profit colleges are doing the hard work of forming a class-based identity around debt as opposed to work or income. The broader cultural conversation about student debt, to which free college plans are a response, sets the stage for that kind of work. The good of those conversations outweighs for me the limited democratization potential of free college.

14

Don't Blame Capitalism for Surging Student Debt

Doug McCullough and Brooke Medina

Doug McCullough is Director of Lone Star Policy Institute. Brooke Medina is communications director at Civitas Institute in NC.

In the following viewpoint Doug McCullough and Brooke Medina argue that, contrary to some popular assertions, capitalism is not the reason that the United States is in a student debt crisis. The authors offer that free tuition to state universities is not the answer, as taxpayers would become responsible for picking up those costs. Instead, they argue, state legislatures should set public college rates. Applying market-based innovations to state colleges could expand access to more individuals without saddling them with crippling debt.

American college graduates are suffering financially under the weight of $1.5 trillion of student loan debt. The bulk of that debt stems from worrisome federal student loan practices and ballooning state tuition costs. Approximately 75 percent of college students attend a state university or college with tuition rates set by legislatures or state institutions. Over 85 percent of student loans are generated under the federal student loan program. In the past three decades, tuition at state colleges has increased by 313 percent.

Oddly, some seem to blame "capitalism" for the student loan predicament. Ray Dalio, billionaire investor, cited massive student debt loads in a recent article that made the case for reforming capitalism. Presidential Candidate John Hickenlooper penned an op-ed for the *Wall Street Journal* boldly proclaiming he is running for president to save capitalism. The very first point in his argument is that (public) high school education doesn't provide adequate training for the modern economy. Anecdotally, we have heard the federal student loan predicament conflated with capitalism.

The Hardship Is Real

The pain of student debt is real. Sadly, there are many adults burdened by thousands of dollars in loan debt. Khalilah Beecham-Watkins, a first-generation college student and young mom, is one of many who feels as if they're a prisoner to student loan debt. Khalilah has been working to pay down her $80,000 debt while helping her husband tackle his own loan obligations. In an interview last year, she said, "I feel like I'm drowning."

As is well-reported, many young adults feel like Khalilah. In the United States, the average student loan debt is more than $37,000. As unsettling as that figure is, some graduates face even higher debt loads. About five percent of degree earners have student loan debt totaling $100,000 or more. Stories like Khalilah's need to be told so that students don't flippantly take on crushing debt without recognizing the gravity of such a decision.

This significant debt load is exacerbated by the fact that many graduates are finding it difficult to find well-paying jobs, which has spiraled into incredibly high rates of loan delinquency: More than one out of every 10 loan recipients is unable to keep up with payments. The Brookings Institute estimates that nearly 40 percent of borrowers will default by 2023. These are sobering statistics, and it's important that borrowers be fully aware of the risks and benefits associated with debt of all kinds, including student loans.

The Benefits of Investing in a College Degree

Despite the burden that comes with debt, there are undeniable long-term benefits to earning a degree. In our skills-based economy, it is no surprise that a person with a bachelor's degree will earn significantly more than a person with only a high school diploma. It has been estimated that a bachelor's degree increases a person's average lifetime earnings by $2.8 million.

And the more degrees someone holds, the more their earning potential increases. Studies indicate that earning a graduate degree could triple a person's expected income. But in the near-term, the financial stress of loan delinquency, deferred consumption, and lower net worth is real.

While the buck ultimately stops with each of us when it comes to our own financial decisions, the student loan quagmire is chiefly the product of federal policy. Federal laws prohibiting sound commercial lending practices and states setting tuition rates high enough to guarantee they're able to absorb all the federal money they can are complicit in this widespread problem.

Bad Diagnoses Lead to Bad Prescriptions

Rather than addressing the underlying problems of federal financial aid and rising public college tuition, politicians like Senators Elizabeth Warren or Bernie Sanders are offering politically expedient ideas. Sen. Warren proposes debt cancellation of up to $50,000 to more than 42 million people.

Sen. Warren's plan would eliminate debt for 75% of borrowers with student loans, and federal funding to ensure students attend state college for free. But nothing in life is free. Warren's sleight-of-hand doesn't make existing debt or future tuition magically disappear. Rather those costs are passed on to taxpayers. And since college graduates earn roughly twice as much as high school graduates and can expect to be in higher tax brackets, guess who would be paying the taxes for Sen. Warren's plan.

Why Federal Loans Are Not Like Commercial Loans

To understand the federal student loan mess, it is necessary to understand some details about the loans that are at the center of the issue. The federal government provides a few types of loans, but the largest share of student debt comes from subsidized and unsubsidized federal loans.

In the case of a subsidized loan, the Department of Education pays the interest on the loan while the student is in school and for six months thereafter. A student can qualify for this type of loan whether or not they are creditworthy or have the ability to repay the loan.

In typical commercial lending, a bank would not offer a loan to an individual who didn't hold a reasonable promise of being able and willing to repay it. This harkens back to 2008 when the US housing market collapsed because of irresponsible lending practices and the belief that everyone—no matter their financial situation—should own a home. It should be no surprise, then, that some economists predict a similar implosion of the student loan market. In other contexts, this would be called predatory lending.

The State's Role in Tuition Inflation

The second contributor to these financial aid troubles is ballooning state college tuition rates. State legislatures and state institutions set public college rates, so these state officials should be held accountable to provide lower-cost alternatives. One lower-cost alternative to traditional on-campus programs would be to offer a basic skills-based college curriculum online at-cost, i.e., based on the marginal cost of providing downloadable lecture videos and similar programming.

While the total cost to a student of an online degree currently tends to be less than a traditional degree, the tuition is often the same. By offering video of select classes, schools could unlock the value of their existing educational resources and expand access to more students. However, state schools are largely immune from market discipline, which encourages cost-cutting and leveraging economies of scale. Instead of reducing operating costs and tuition prices, state schools soak up the flow of federal loan dollars.

On the finance side, state universities could offer their own alternative to federal student loans. Take, for instance, the market-oriented model of Purdue University and offer income sharing agreements (ISAs). Income sharing agreements allow consumers to pay off a debt by sharing a portion of the student's income with the lender for a set number of years. Instead of a loan, ISAs allow investors to take "equity" in a student's future earnings for a period of time.

The problem with the financial aid predicament is that market discipline has been eliminated from state college education and federal financial aid. Public colleges aren't going to be privatized and run like for-profit businesses any time soon. However, by applying market-based innovations and lessons from the private sector to state colleges, it may be possible to expand access to state college, offer alternative financing arrangements (like income sharing agreements), and reduce the cost of college through technology and economies of scale.

15

There Is No Such Thing as a Free Lunch

William E. Fleischmann

William E. Fleischmann is an economist and financial professional with more than thirty years of experience in banking, insurance, and healthcare. Fleischmann has a passion for economic history and, in particular, the extensive harm done by minimum wage laws.

In the following viewpoint William E. Fleischmann argues that "free" college tuition will be anything but, since someone has to be responsible for the expense. The author uses the example of England's struggling higher education structure to show the downfalls of government-funded universities and notes that perhaps our problem is not as profound as some say it is. The real problem might be expectations and feelings of entitlement. After all, students have a choice whether or not to take on this debt.

Presidential candidates and campaigns have been offering "a chicken in every pot" for at least 90 years now, but this election cycle seems to be all about offering more "free" stuff than the other candidates. Some have even gone so far as to claim it's not a problem that the government prints money to cover such things, as if the concept of Modern Monetary Theory (MMT, or, more accurately, Mindless Magical Thinking) makes it okay.

"Elizabeth Warren's Plan to Eliminate Student Debt Is Worse Than You Think," by William E. Fleischmann, Foundation for Economic Education, https://fee.org/articles/elizabeth-warren-s-plan-to-eliminate-student-debt-is-worse-than-you-think/ May 3, 2019. Licensed under CC-BY 4.0.

One point relevant to this discussion is that MMT is based on the premise that government can allocate resources more efficiently than the alternative had their exercise of monopoly power over the currency not taken place—a premise without a single example in all of human history.

The latest salvo in the Free Stuff Wars comes from Elizabeth Warren and her plan to cancel (most) student loans and offer free college to everyone. Some have even suggested, most notably the Levy Institute at Bard College (affiliated with self-described socialist Joseph Stiglitz), that such a plan would "super-charge the economy." The premise, as we shall see, is absurd on its face. Surely, this is an effective way to woo millennials with college debt. As George Bernard Shaw noted, "A government which robs Peter to pay Paul can always count on the support of Paul," but that hardly makes it a sound idea economically.

How Did We Get Here?

There are a number of reasons college debt has ballooned, and understanding them is key to determining how best to address the "problem." The realities haven't changed since Thomas Sowell wrote on these topics more than a decade ago.

First, there's simply supply and demand. According to the National Center for Education Statistics, enrollment in all Title IV institutions, while down somewhat in the post-recession period (attributed to lower birth rates), is still up 36.3 percent from 1995 levels. Over the same period, the percentage of the population with a college degree has risen from 20.2 percent for women and 26 percent for men to 35.3 percent for women and 34.6 percent for men.

Today, nearly 70 percent of recent high school graduates are enrolled in college. Unsurprisingly, tuition and fees have skyrocketed. The powers that be have responded by throwing ever more money at the problem.

Unfortunately, that has only made the problem worse. As economists David Lucca, Taylor Nadauld, and Karen Shen found, roughly 60 cents of every dollar in federal credit expansion for tuition goes only to increasing tuition. No wonder spending on higher education in the US already exceeds that of many countries with supposedly "free" college. An earlier study found that

> changes to the Federal Student Loan Program (FSLP) ... alone generate[d] a 102% tuition increase" between 1987 and 2010, "which more than accounts for the 78% increase seen in the data.

In addition, there are already no less than 13 student loan forgiveness programs already in effect, most of which require nominal payments for 10 to 20 years before any balance is forgiven (a major disincentive to balance reduction). The *New York Times* recently provided a perfect example, citing the case of Samantha and Justin Morgan, who are on an "income-based" repayment plan and will see their loan balance continually rise until the balance is ultimately forgiven. You can't significantly increase loan outlays, implement policies that hinder repayment, and then honestly act surprised that balances soar.

Who Reaps the Benefits?

Elizabeth Warren's plan has been fairly described as a "bailout for the elite," as the top 25 percent of households by income hold almost half of all student debt and as the cost would fall on all taxpayers when about two-thirds of American adults have no college degree, not to mention the 3-in-10 students who leave college debt-free (if you planned ahead or stepped up and paid your debt off, this scheme is a slap in the face).

But, as the Lucca-Nadlaud-Shen study makes clear, the real beneficiaries are the educational institutions that enjoy the benefit of more money being added to the system without a change in supply.

What Are the Consequences?

Cost: As with health care, and as we've already seen with tuition, you never really see just how expensive something can be until it's "free." The initial cost of debt cancellation, as Warren herself points out, is $640 billion. Then, of course, she suggests that the tab to taxpayers for "free" college will be $1.25 trillion over the next 10 years. Even that staggering figure, however, does not take into account what we already know happens when federal money is funneled toward tuition.

If the 60 cents on the dollar figure holds—and there's no reason to suspect otherwise—it would take $2.08 trillion just to meet the students Warren has taken into account. And then there's the demand side of the equation. Of the 30 percent of high school graduates not enrolling in college under current conditions, how many does one suppose would enroll when college is "free"?

This conundrum inevitably leads to rationing. As Ryan McMaken notes, "In the real world, no scarce resource can be both open to all, and also very inexpensive." This explains why countries with "free tuition" often have a lower—often materially lower—percentage of college graduates.

Quality: It's difficult to argue that the highest quality higher education in the world is in the United States due to accident rather than due to the retention of economic incentives. The elimination of those incentives can hardly have anything but a material detrimental effect on the quality of education provided. The experience in England until the late 1990s is particularly relevant.

Free college caused "quality to decline and socioeconomic inequality to rise." As noted by Preston Cooper in *Forbes*,

> *England's experience highlights a fundamental problem with a government role in higher education: If universities rely more on government than students for funding, the level of investment in higher education hinges on the whims of politicians rather than the needs of students.*

What Those Claiming Economic Benefits Get Wrong

All of the claims of economic benefit from both the elimination of student loan debt and the offering of "free" college boil down to the assumption that resources would be better allocated if only students didn't have this debt to service. They point, for example, to lower rates of home ownership among those under 30 (conveniently glossing over the fact that the same falloff was seen for both those with no college and those graduates with no college debt), but even there, the evidence is mixed.

While the consensus is that "American youth hav[e] accommodated tuition shocks not by forgoing schooling, but instead by amassing more debt," perhaps explaining the "decline in homeownership for 28-to-30-year-olds over 2007–15," the fundamental point missed by those favoring debt forgiveness is simple choice.

Those incurring student debt did not have it imposed upon them. Rather, debt was incurred because the borrower determined that it was in their interests to incur that debt in order to obtain the benefits of higher education. They did so knowing it would mean that those resources would not be available to spend on other things.

Certainly, sometimes those decisions were in error, but, particularly for those not majoring in ethnic studies, fine arts, or philosophy, by and large, the benefits of taking on that debt to obtain a higher education still materially outweigh the costs. As one economist noted in 2014,

> The typical student holds debt that is well below the lifetime benefits of a college education. The typical student borrower is not "under water," as were many homeowners during the mortgage crisis.

From an economic perspective, there is no reason to second-guess the decision-making process of those who benefit most from the educational services being purchased and, in order for there to be a real economic benefit from expending taxpayer resources to allow those borrowers to expend resources elsewhere, it would have to be demonstrated that those decisions, overall, were wrong in the first place.

16

Doing the Work You Love May Not Pay Off

Elizabeth Verklan

Elizabeth Verklan is Assistant Professor of women, gender, and sexuality studies at Cottey College. Her first book, Objects of Desire: Transnational Feminism, Feminist Inquiry, and Global Fashion, *under contract with University of Illinois Press, examines how sweatshops are framed and represented in and to the United States.*

Many students take on burdensome loans as investments in their future. Nearly two-thirds of that debt is taken on by women, who earn more bachelor's degrees in the United States than men. The idea is that the education funded by the loan will end up paying off in the end. However, college degrees don't always lead to well-paying jobs. In some industries, such as the fashion industry, unpaid internships are the only way to get a foot in the door. Interns are overworked and unpaid, and they often ultimately don't see the financial returns on their loans.

In 2017, education debt in the US reached $1.4 trillion dollars. While this exorbitant sum is shared among 44 million borrowers, it is not shared equally. Examining data from a 2016 study produced by the US Department of Education, the American Association of University Women (hereafter, AAUW) report that while 2007–08 male college graduates were able to secure full-time employment to pay off their student loans, their female counterparts were not. The report states: "Between 2009 and 2012, men who graduated in the 2007–08 school year paid off an average of 44% of their student debt, while women in that group managed to pay off only 33% of their student debt." This discrepancy is troubling given that more women, 53%, compared with 39% of their male counterparts, are putting more of their salaries towards student debt repayment, which means that these women are "less able to save for retirement, buy a car, or invest in a home." The AAUW attributes this discrepancy to the gender pay gap, and emphasizes that the inability to pay back student debt is worst for Latinas (who had paid back 3 percent at the time of the study) and African-American women (9 percent), while white women (37 percent) and Asian-American women (61 percent) were considerably higher, albeit still trailing their male counterparts.

As Maurizio Lazzarato and Andrew Ross argue, debt has become a significant social force, shaping the terms with which individuals understand themselves and society. At the same time, Lazzarato, Ross, and Michael Hardt assert that waged work has become increasingly precarious and immaterial in nature. Building on this scholarship, this paper examines the relationship between student debt and the changing terrain of work in US culture, while attending to how these shifts mark a specifically gendered, racialized phenomenon. While Lazzarato, Ross, and Hardt provide compelling arguments regarding the nature of work and debt in contemporary capitalism, they do not address how the proliferation of immaterial labor marks what Angela McRobbie describes as the "feminization" of the labor force. As McRobbie observes, increasing precarity and immateriality dovetail with the "feminization of work … the expansion of possibilities for women's employment across many countries and particularly in the affluent countries where there had been a strong feminist movement in the 1960s." As McRobbie argues, "The nature of work in a post-Fordist economy favored the large skill pool and the flexibility of the female workforce," leading to a growth in female workers within the creative industries marked by precarity and immateriality, such as fashion. In this way, both the demographics of the labor force as well as the labor itself became feminized, because the very work becoming "increasingly precarious, and under compensated" was, and is, explicitly "reliant on 'soft' skills such as communication, affect and cognition." In other words, the feminization of work also entails the proliferation of those skills presumed "natural" to female persons (e.g., service, nurturance, and communication), but also long associated with the pink collar professions. However, this is not to assert a gender essentialism, but rather to acknowledge how modes of laboring historically associated with women (e.g., emotional, service-oriented, boundary-less, and unwaged) now characterize the labor of many immaterial workers. As Christina Morini argues, "in cognitive capitalism precariousness, mobility, and fragmentation become constituent elements of the work of all persons irrespective of gender. The model advanced is pliable, hyper-flexible, and in this sense, it draws on the baggage of female experience." Thus, to discuss the feminization of work is to acknowledge that in the post-Fordist era, not only are women participating in fields like the culture industries at an unprecedented rate, but the immaterial labor they undertake is feminizing in that it re-enforces a gender structure wherein woman-identified persons are disadvantaged via precarious employment. The significance of gender to understanding immateriality and student debt is especially worthy of consideration then because woman-identified persons are further in debt, are less likely to secure the kind of employment after graduation to pay it back, and (as I discuss below) are over-represented in those labor forms that remain very low-waged, if waged at all.

At the same time, race also occupies a central role in understanding the gendered machinations of student indebtedness. As the figures regarding student indebtedness above highlight, debt repayment is most difficult for Latinas and African-American women, while it remains less so for white and Asian-American women. Thus, to speak of gendered indebtedness is to speak of racialized, gendered indebtedness, as the persons most impacted by student debt are women of color. This aspect of student indebtedness is not unrelated to the feminization of work. As Minh-Ha Pham outlines in her discussion of the invisible labors of Asian fashion superbloggers, "the racialization of women's work has also benefitted white women" (emphasis added). As Evelyn Nakano Glenn argues, the nineteenth-century "cult of domesticity" that structured gender relations depended on the invisible domestic labors of women (and men) of color, effectively establishing a racial stratification within the realm of women's work. Thus, while the feminization of work "draws on the baggage of female experience," it necessarily draws on the historical realities of women's work that have produced racial stratifications among women, of which white women have benefitted. The historical legacies of these stratifications continue in numerous forms of gendered, racialized labors that effectively reproduce a racial hierarchy wherein economically privileged, white women consume and benefit from the labors of women of color. I examine the figure of the fashion intern because she illustrates how such racial stratifications among women are reproduced and intensified via student indebtedness. Additionally, as I outline below, the fashion intern is a particularly apt example because she highlights how racial stratifications within culture industries such as fashion are perpetuated.

Examining this phenomenon, I ask how the ideological imperative to 'do what you love' contributes to the gendered workings of indebtedness. "Do what you love, and love what you do" is often presented as a form of spiritual guidance. For instance, in one of the more famous pronouncements of the "do what you love" ethos, in his 2005 Stanford graduation address, the late Steve Jobs advised graduating students "to find what you love" because, "the only way to do great work is to love what you do." As a life ethos, "do what you love" suggests that exploitation is something that one can opt out of, because if one loves their work, then not only are they not exploited, but they are not working. In a

2014 *Jacobin* magazine article shared over 65,000 times on social media (and published as a book in 2015), author Miya Tokumitsu argues that the discourse of "do what you love" bears considerable advantages to capitalism, while hurting workers everywhere. As Tokumitsu asserts, "According to this way of thinking, labor is not something one does for compensation, but an act of self-love." In this analysis, doing what one loves ensures spiritual fulfillment, albeit with adequate benefits and compensation perceived as incidentals, rather than necessities for survival.

Taken in the context of mass student debt, I pursue the following questions: What kinds of work are made possible, or impossible through the imperative to "do what one loves"? How does the imperative to "do what you love" intensify inequity along economic, racial, and gendered lines, especially within the context of mass debt? And, more specifically, how might the directive to "love" one's work, to warrant work null through "love," mark a particularly gendered manifestation of indebtedness? Pursuing these questions, I examine the figure of the fashion intern, whose gendered, culturally unrecognizable labor is a part of the broader proliferation of precarious labor forms marked by "instability, the absence of legal contracts (of employment abiding by legal standards) lack of protection and social benefits, lack of collective agreement of employment, and low wages" that permeate and characterize most of the culture industries in the current moment. The fashion intern is one of the most iconic yet culturally unrecognizable fashion workers, and I assert that this misrecognition is because the fashion intern "loves" what she does, and thus does not work. I examine the fashion intern in order to think about how the gender and racial inequities evident in student debt collude with the feminization of cultural work, effecting a gendered, racialized form of indebtedness.

Examining the figure of the fashion intern then is an attempt to illustrate two important aspects crucial to understanding the structure of student debt and immaterial labor in the current moment. The first concerns the way in which immaterial labor, particularly that within the culture industries like fashion, is increasingly gendered feminine. This gendering occurs through the feminization of work that entails an increase in woman-identified persons undertaking these labors, but also the way in which this labor is characterized by its flexibility, adaptability, emotion work, and lack of a wage. The figure of the fashion intern is exemplary in this regard, as her labor, despite being crucial to the operations of fashion, remains culturally unrecognizable and unwaged. The second aspect concerns how the combination of mass student indebtedness and unpaid internships effectively prohibits women of color specifically, and indebted students generally, from entering fields within the culture industries such as fashion. As a 2012 study undertaken by *The Chronicle of Higher Ed[ucation]* illustrates, internships remain the primary route with which recent graduates and/or new workers gain entry to their desired professions. Internships throughout the culture industries, however, tend to be unpaid, demanding work that is economically prohibitive for any person carrying a significant debt load. Examining the figure of the fashion intern demonstrates how labor that—for all intents and purposes—exploits its workers and is compelled for free, nonetheless simultaneously acts as a means by which to bar the most economically vulnerable and historically underrepresented groups in these very industries. Thus, while the figure of the fashion intern highlights the feminization of immaterial work, she also exemplifies the ways in which "the categories of free labor and the various forms of subjugated labor—including slave labor, indentured labor, and sweated labor—are economic expressions of racial and gendered logics." Examining the figure of the fashion intern, then, is a means with which to articulate both the racial and gendered logics that underpin her exploitation but also the ways in which the racial inequities that permeate the fashion industry are perpetuated.

[...]

The Politics of Student Debt

As the AAUW reports, women possess "nearly two-thirds of the outstanding student debt in the US." On the surface, this imbalance along gender lines reflects the changes in student population in higher education over the last sixty years. Women now earn more than half (57 percent) of bachelor's degrees in the US, and between 1976 and 2014 the total number of undergraduate students identifying as not-white "more than doubled from 16 percent to 42 percent." However, these shifts in student population cannot account for the reality of student debt inequity. While the median household income has stagnated since 1976, the "median cost of college attendance has more than doubled since then." This soaring cost of college attendance has unequally impacted women; women take on an average of 44 percent of debt for undergraduate education, compared to 39 percent for men. As the AAUW notes, this discrepancy between debt load is exacerbated by the gender pay gap, because: "Women working full time with college degrees make 26 percent less than their male counterparts," which means less money to put towards repayment of student loans.

For women of color, the rising cost of college attendance and gender pay gap is most severe. As noted in the AAUW report, wealth in the US is distributed along racial lines, as white and Asian families tend to have much higher incomes and accrued familial wealth than black or Latino families. These discrepancies in total accrued wealth means that black and Latino students have less economic support from family members, and are more likely to cover the total costs of their education as individuals. These differences are reflected in the AAUW's research: "[T]he typical black woman who graduated with a bachelor's degree in 2011–12 did so with about $29,000 in student loans while black men averaged $25,000 … Asian graduates had the lowest debt, averaging about $11,000 in debt at graduation." While black students—regardless of gender—share the bulk of student debt, it is black women who comprise the most indebted on average. As the AAUW states, "Women—especially women of color—are most likely to experience difficulties, 34 percent of all women and 57 percent of black women who were repaying student loans report[ed] that they had been unable to meet essential expenses within the last year."

While the gains in diversity in higher education are positive outcomes of the legislative policies and political movements of the previous century, in order to be truly transformative, they must entail actual gains post-graduation. The inability to meet basic needs because one has obtained an advanced degree does not reflect an actual step towards equity in higher education; particularly because it is the very students held up as proof of change (i.e., students of color, women, first-generation students, women of color) who are struggling in this endeavor. Many of these students are also nontraditional students: parents of dependent children (including single parents), students financially independent of their parents, veterans, students re-entering college after significant time away (and thus often older), part-time students, and students working full-time while enrolled are increasingly entering post-secondary institutions. Many of these nontraditional students are "disproportionately women, people of color, and first-generation college students." Additionally, many of these students face hurdles to completing their college education that traditional students do not: balancing work and class schedules, finding affordable, dependent childcare, and facing interpersonal and psychological difficulties succeeding in an atmosphere catering to a much younger, childless, non-working student population. For single parents in particular (now more than 26 percent of all degree-seeking post-secondary students in the US), completing a college degree will pose the most difficulty. As the AAUW states: "Most student parents—69 percent—are low income, defined as at or below 200 percent of the federal poverty level," many of whom are also single parents (54 percent), and women (71 percent). Students with dependent children are more likely to take on larger amounts of debt, and take a longer amount of time to finish their degree programs (which also tends to entail a higher debt load). However, completing a degree program, regardless of debt load, is far better than leaving without a degree. As the AAUW report outlines, students who leave college before completing are more likely to default on their student loans, and it tends to be nontraditional students who leave college before completing their programs.

There is much to be gleaned from the AAUW's research on student debt, but perhaps the most significant to the present study is the way in which student debt works towards reinforcing existing social hierarchies through the very promise of transforming them. In this regard, the AAUW report affirms much of the theoretical insights garnered from recent literature concerning indebtedness. In his 2012 text, "The Making of the Indebted Man," Lazzarato argues that the debtor-creditor relationship "intensifies mechanisms of exploitation and domination at every level of society," via a slow yet consistent tax on one's future wages and possibilities. As the AAUW report highlights, student debt works towards a calcification of the very structural and social inequities higher education is often touted as transcending, such as socioeconomic class. Taken as an intensifier of exploitation and inequity, student debt succeeds in this endeavor, as the students entering college with the least social and economic capital stand to leave with the most debt, and demonstrate the most difficulty repaying it. For example, this function of student debt is quite evident when considering the profitability of loan defaults, the most lucrative opportunities for creditors. As noted above, nontraditional students are not only most likely to leave college before obtaining a degree, but as such, they are also the most likely to default. In this way, the very students already facing barriers to degree completion (such as childcare, ageism, work-school balance, etc.) become the most profitable to the student-debt system through their failure. Thus, rather than enabling more students to obtain a degree once previously prohibitive, student debt has expanded the opportunities for exploitation and domination already in place.

In addition to the intensification of material inequities, the debt economy entails a re-figuration of subjectivity itself. As

Lazzarato outlines, the predominance of the debtor-creditor relation in capitalist society comprises a material (i.e., economic indebtedness and thus a diminishment of one's overall wages) as well as a subjective component. As Lazzarato states, "It is debt and the creditor-debtor relationship that make up the subjective paradigm of modern-day capitalism, in which 'labor' is coupled with 'work on the self', in which economic activity and the ethico-political activity of producing the subject go hand in hand." It is this "work on the self" that is so significant to understanding student debt; accepted as a necessary burden in order to obtain economic and social capital, student debt differs from other kinds of debt in that it is most often framed as a means to a better life. Taking on student debt means that one is taking steps towards a better future, even if that future is compromised by rising debt load. As Ross argues, while the subjective component of student debt includes individuated kinds of violence, such as depression, suicide, and divorce, it simultaneously guides the means of protest, as publicly revealing and "owning" one's debt did during the Occupy protests of 2011. This personalized aspect of debt is quite evident in the AAUW study, as a significant portion of women—especially black women—reported "very high levels of stress about repayment." In sum, the subjective power of debt remains, and when taken in the context of a shifting terrain of work, bears relevance to understanding why an ethos of "do what you love" contributes to gendered indebtedness. Namely, taken in the context of mass debt and precarious employment, as a spiritual and professional ethos, "do what you love" suggests that work—with or without a wage—is simply enough. As Lazzarato argues, as both an economically material and subjectifying experience, debt reconfigures the ways in which individuals perceive waged labor. Because debt represents a deprivation on future time and money, the substance and meaning in waged work shifts, particularly for those kinds of employment necessarily entailing debt. Speaking to this, Lazzarato states, "The dedication, the subjective motivation, and the work on the self preached by management since the 1980s have become an injunction to take upon oneself the costs of economic and financial disaster." Lazzarato's comments are significant because they point towards the ways in which the injunction to take on debt intersects with ideological imperatives to better oneself, and live one's best life, regardless of actual material improvements to one's overall well-being. In the next section I suggest that the ethos of "do what you love" provides the "injunction to take upon oneself the costs of economic and financial disaster" by sustaining prolonged precarious employment.

[...]

Fashion Interns and Free Labor

Fashion is not possible without free labor. As Lauren Sherman, writing on the industry website *Fashionista* states, "If we don't have unpaid assistants working on set, or in the office, magazines wouldn't get published, film wouldn't get developed, and fashion shows wouldn't run so smoothly." These "assistants" Sherman mentions are interns: individuals who fill positions within fashion brands, design houses and fashion magazines, under the guise that they will receive professional tutelage and skills, with the promise of a job upon its completion. However, these promises are rarely fulfilled. As the now more than thirty lawsuits filed since 2010 evidence, intern labor most typically does not lead to a paid position but rather another internship, and the "skills" one acquires during these stints are most often the reproductive labor necessary to maintaining any corporate entity or business: answering phones, relaying messages, maintaining emails, organizing and cleaning the offices, running errands, and other administrative tasks. However, as Sherman's quote highlights, despite the crucial function this labor provides, it remains unwaged.

The phenomenon of the fashion intern is part of the broader proliferation of precarious labor forms marked by "instability, the absence of legal contracts (of employment abiding by legal standards), lack of protection and social benefits, [and] lack of collective agreement of employment, and low wages." In a 2010 Economic Policy Institute report on the labor of interns, researchers Kathryn Anne Edwards and Alexander Hertel-Fernandez identify the 2008 recession as a turning point in intern labor, as, post-recession, corporations move towards replacing waged-workers with the free, or virtually free, labor of interns. This trend points towards the broader austerity measures enacted in the wake of the 2008 recession. The proliferation of precarious labor forms, such as interns, adjuncts, freelancers, and other independent-contract workers, are a symptom of a larger shift made possible by neoliberal reforms and the dismantling of what little security was attached to labor prior to the 2008 recession. While no one keeps a precise count of how many paid and/or unpaid internships exist at a given moment, a 2008 National Association of Colleges and Employers report found fifty percent of graduating college students had held internships, a drastic increase when compared to a Northwestern University study that evidenced a mere seventeen percent in 1992. As Ross Perlin argues in *Intern Nation: How to Earn Nothing and Learn Little in the Brave New Economy*, the proliferation of this labor form has effectively become "a mainstream experience after the recession began," and as Andrew Ross asserts, the very waged and salary positions held out as promises to interns remain "nice work if you can get it."

While intern labor is utilized across the culture industries, the fashion industry stands as the most iconic. This iconicity is due in large part to the numerous television shows (not to mention films and magazine profiles) of this worker. It is, as Annemarie Strassel observes, a "glamorized form of labor" that remains culturally unrecognizable because of this. Several reality television shows emerging over the last ten years have specifically centered on the figure of the fashion intern: *Running in Heels* (2009), *Kell on Earth* (2010), *The Rachel Zoe Project* (2008–13), *The Fashionista Diaries* (2007), and *The City* (2008–10), a spin-off of another hit reality television series *The Hills* (2006–10). In all of these productions, a young person (usually a feminine woman but also sometimes a feminine man) travels to a big city in order to "pay their dues" at a leading fashion company. The audience follows their misadventures and mishaps while they struggle to "make it" in the industry. Unclear, however, is what exactly constitutes "making it." In *The City* for instance, the show's overarching narrative follows the main character, Whitney Port, concluding her internship with Diane Von Furstenberg with a position at *Elle* magazine, and then selling a clothing line to Bergdorf Goodman via a successful fashion show in Bryant Park during New York City's notoriously competitive and prohibitively expensive Fashion Week. Not only is this narrative arc implausible for most every other intern, but it elides terribly the ways in which Port's lifestyle is impossible based on the incomes and work schedules of actual interns. Further, this narrative arc reframes Port's familial background as irrelevant to her success. Port's familial wealth and social capital warranted her inclusion in the reality television show *The Hills* (that followed a wealthy, white set of teenagers in Orange County, California), which led to her role in *The City*. *The City's* portrayal of Port, both documentary realist in its aesthetic and entirely implausible, renders the very factors that guaranteed her success (i.e., familial wealth and social networks that include television producers) irrelevant, and reframes her rise within the fashion industry as fueled by her "love" of fashion.

In contrast to Port's implausible account is the case of Diana Wang. The case that served as the basis for a 2012 class-action lawsuit, Wang's story both reproduces and departs from the archetypal narrative presented throughout pop culture:

In August 2011 Xuedan "Diana" Wang began her "dream" position as the "head accessories intern" at the legendary fashion magazine *Harper's Bazaar* after graduating from Ohio State. Upending her life in Colombus, she moved to New York City only to find herself working as many as fifty-five hours a week without pay. She supervised eight other interns, ran menial errands, and hauled bags of clothes between publicity firms. On some days Wang was unable to eat lunch until 4pm and worked as late as 10pm with no break for dinner. Five months after her internship began, Wang concluded her work as a glorified messenger service for the magazine with no job offer and little professional experience that might help her gain a foothold in the fashion industry. It was her seventh unpaid internship.

Diana's story is unfortunately not unique. In fact, it is quite similar to another fashion intern's story, Lauren Ballinger, who in her last semester at the American University of Paris "saved one credit before graduating to use toward an internship at *W*," a leading US fashion magazine. "Ms. Ballinger was paid $12.00 a day to work in *W*'s Accessories Department," working from eight or nine each morning until eight to ten every night, "packing, organizing, and delivering accessories to editors." Further, Ballinger, who took the position as a part of her career training, was not only trained by other interns, and thus did not receive the insider industry training nor the networking opportunities she was promised, but the *W* editors refused to provide Ballinger with a recommendation upon the completion of her internship, effectively withholding from her her last remaining academic credit.

Wang and Ballinger's stories are not exceptional but are symptomatic of a larger trend in compelling free labor from a largely young pool of educated, ambitious individuals. Overwhelmingly, this labor pool across culture industries is female, with 77 percent of the intern labor workforce woman-identified. This aspect of the labor pool not only reflects the ways in which cultural representations of the fashion intern compels young women and feminine-leaning persons to pursue it, but also points to how the skills crucial to creative industries, such as flexibility, creativity, and an aesthetic sensibility, is gendered largely feminine, whether a male-identified or female-identified person performs it. Speaking to the topic of feminine labor, Donna Haraway suggests that:

> *To be feminized is to be made extremely vulnerable; able to be disassembled, reassembled, exploited as reserve labor force; seen less as workers than as servers; subjected to time arrangements*

on and off the paid job that make a mockery of a limited work day; leading an existence that always borders on the obscene, or out of place.

The labor required of interns—free, reproductive in nature, and invisible, with erratic and overly long work hours—is overwhelmingly feminine. As Minh-ha Pham observes, the feminine labor that fashion requires contributes to the perceived triviality of fashion, which works towards its dismissal as an object of study or critique. I suggest that the gender of fashion is crucial to the perpetuation of the kind of labor exploitation characterized by the fashion intern, because in its triviality, invisibility, and lack of a wage it is rationalized as not 'real' labor and thus not 'real' exploitation, and also because the persons doing it (i.e., young, feminine persons) are culturally expected to "love" this work. In effect, this labor is naturalized in ways that render it non-work.

In addition to gender, the labor of interns reproduces the racial hierarchies evident in the AAUW's research regarding student debt: Latinas and black women are largely absent, both in media representations and high-profile intern lawsuits. This lack of representation points to the ways in which the feminization of work in culture industries works towards the exclusion of the most indebted: Latinas and black women. In this way, the "do what you love" ethos that justifies the precarity exemplary in the figure of the fashion intern also legitimates the racial exclusions of the fashion industry broadly. "Do what you love" is not then merely a means with which to reorient workers to a precarious labor market, but a way to reframe the structural exclusions that reproduce industries like fashion as predominantly white. In this way, the unpaid internship—of which the fashion intern is but one—is not only a feminized job, but a racialized one.

To be clear, while most of the intern workers within the fashion industry are either completing degrees (and the internship constitutes a portion of their education) or possess one, not all intern workers are young, idealistic twenty-somethings. For many individuals working as interns, their hopes of obtaining "success" are diluted through a seemingly endless series of internships, effecting what Alex Williams terms "a permanent intern underclass" whose inability to secure waged employment is upheld through programs forever holding out the promise of a job with a paycheck. Wang's story states that her position at *Harper's* was her seventh, while in another high-profile case (that also lead to a lawsuit), Eric Glatt, who holds a Masters degree in Business Administration in addition to a Bachelor of Arts, was forty-four and had just finished his fourth internship when he began organizing on behalf of interns. This age difference makes sense when considering the larger context within which it exists: namely, the dissolution of paid positions within the culture industries and their replacement with unpaid interns. Doing work within the culture industry (whether fashion, film, or music) means doing it for free, or very nearly so. This phenomenon stands in stark contrast to the promises extended by the internship itself: a future with a paycheck. Internships are held out as temporary stopovers on one's way to something bigger and better, when in reality, the internship is a mode of work that is both temporary and short-lived, exemplifying precarious working conditions with little end in sight. This exact reality is captured in the case of Alec Dudson, who after completing several sequential internships, at 29 started *Intern* magazine, a biannual glossy that provides articles, tips, and inspiration for what *The New York Times* tellingly refers to as "the faceless drones who keep the style industries humming." Dudson's venture is not alone; there is *FindSpark*, a New York jobs network for recent graduates that provides meet-ups and events with themes such as "follow your passion," and "your ideal brand" that "draw hundreds." There are also several blogs detailing the daily toils of interns in various industries: *Life of an Investment Banking Summer Slave*, *Anonymous Production Assistant* (for interns working within the film and television industries), *Intern-Anonymous* (for all interns), and most relevant to the present study, *Fashion Intern Problems* and *The Devil Pays Nada* (for fashion interns). These cultural phenomena not only point towards the widespread proliferation of this labor form, but also towards its suspended, if not indefinite, nature. For Glatt, who is a founding member of the group Intern Labor Rights, internship labor operates as "an institutionalized form of wage theft." In this way, many individuals express feeling "trapped" in a cycle that, the longer one is in it seems all the more difficult to leave because one has already put in "dues" towards that elusive future job.

This aspect of their status as workers is exacerbated by the fact that most intern workers are already fearful of speaking up or expressing grievances because of the competitive and tenuous nature of their position. This level of competition is no more apparent than in the world of high fashion, when in 2012, thousands of individuals bid through an online auction for a chance to intern, and specifically, work for free at Chanel, Balenciaga, and Valentino. It is this level of competition made possible by both the post-recession hiring practices, but also the ideology of doing what one loves, that maintains the pervasive belief that should one leave there is always already someone else willing to fill your space. As Edwards and Hertel-Fernandez outline in their study, "The crucial role of internships in obtaining later employment and the highly competitive market for placement means that no one student has an incentive to report to their employer, even in cases of blatant abuses, since another student will readily work for free." As one former intern worker, Rachel Watson, stated when discussing her lawsuit against British fashion house Alexander McQueen: "How could I confront my employer at the time when they held all the cards to my future in the industry?" Watson's comment speaks to the way in which the very purpose of the internship—industry affiliation—simultaneously serves as the underlying punitive threat. In other words, by offering one's labor for free in exchange for a promise, one is already at a disadvantage.

This disadvantaged position interns occupy in relation to their employers is structured within the very terms established to prevent their exploitation. Established in 1938, and later strengthened with six guidelines via a 1947 Supreme Court case, the Fair Labor Standards Act (hereafter, FLSA) provides the terms against which the legality of an internship is measured. The guidelines, meant to differentiate between an employee and trainee, do so through the following guidelines: a shared assumption that the labor performed is for vocational and/or educational purposes (and is thus training rather than employment); that the training benefits the trainees; that trainees do not replace regular employees (but work under their supervision); that the employer receive no immediate advantage from the trainee's activities (and may even experience such training as an impediment); that trainees are not entitled to a job upon completion of the training, and that there is a mutual understanding that trainees are not entitled to wages. If all six guidelines are met, then the "employee" is legally considered to be a "trainee," or in this case an intern. However, there are several crucial limits to these guidelines, the first of which concerns the wageless nature of this work. Originally intended to establish guidelines for apprenticeships that were for manual labor and production work, these guidelines cannot and do not account for how the US labor market has changed dramatically, exemplified here in the creative labor necessary to culture industries like fashion. As Edwards and Hertel-Fernandez note, "A serious problem surrounding unpaid interns is [that] they are often not considered employees and therefore are not protected by employment discrimination laws," such as legislation that protects against sexual harassment, and discrimination based on race, age, or physical and/or mental ability. This is because the very statutes that are intended to protect employees in the workplace are established on the grounds of a relationship wherein the employer provides the employee with a wage, the very thing that mediates and defines them as such. Further, these guidelines "permit (and even incentivize) the replacement of regular workers with unpaid college students and recent graduates," because it sanctions the employer's practice of compelling free labor from intern workers under the guise of "educational purposes." The supposed "educational purposes" are evident in the mediating body that most often arranges the internships: university programs that possess corporate contracts with the internship offering agencies. Indeed, it is difficult to imagine any situation wherein free labor is not to the immediate advantage of an employer (or in this case, the educator). It is this aspect (i.e., the "educational purposes" that render the labor unwaged) of the unpaid positions that fosters their growth, because it is always to the employers' advantage to obtain labor for free, rather than having to invest in a waged worker. This leads to what is perhaps the most glaring problem to the proliferation of this labor: the way in which it limits the participation to students who can afford to work for free, "effectively institutionalizing socioeconomic disparities."

The normalization of unpaid internships throughout the culture industries means that these industries—like fashion—are increasingly exclusive, reserved for those with familial and/or industry connections, and the means with which to support unpaid work. As noted in a 2012 report conducted by *The Chronicle of Higher Education*, internships remain the single most important factor when considering a college graduate for employment. However, because student debt is a necessary burden for some students seeking a degree, unpaid internships—and thus some career paths—are not an option. This exclusionary entry to internships has implications regarding the composition of the very culture industries relying on intern labor. As internship servicers such as InternMatch have shown, unpaid internships contribute to the lack of diversity in certain industries. Long criticized for its exclusionary nature, fashion has most recently endured numerous public condemnations concerning structural racism. Considering the industry's reliance on unpaid internships, it is perhaps unsurprising to find that women of color, most prominently Latinas and black women, experience difficulty succeeding in, or gaining entry into the fashion world. Additionally, when considering the ethos of "do what you love," it seems that very few, and perhaps more importantly, very few women of color, are actually able to do so.

What the fashion intern points to then is how the immaterial, precarious labor of the culture industries manifests in highly gendered, racialized ways. Represented as a glamorous lifestyle, the fashion intern typically does not earn wages, nor does she (and she is typically a "she") obtain the waged position she was promised. The fashion intern's labor (like other precarious workers of the culture industries) is feminine in that it remains unwaged and highly flexible, yet performs a socially reproductive function. Indeed, her unwaged labor is crucial to fashion's production. Similarly, when examined in the context of mass debt, the fashion intern is not merely a feminized job but a racialized one, meaning that it perpetuates the whiteness of the fashion industry through its exclusivity (i.e., being able to perform demanding work without a wage). Further, like other precarious labor forms, the fashion intern's labor is compelled and naturalized through the ideology of "do what you love"; because it is work that one "loves," one should perform it for free, and because one "loves" it (and is willing to perform it for free), it is not work but rather an extension of one's highest self. In sum, examining the fashion intern illustrates how the feminization of work and the ethos of "do what you love" collude to disadvantage those most negatively impacted by student debt—Latinas and black women—and also perpetuates the whiteness of the fashion industry itself.

Organizations to Contact

The editors have compiled the following list of organizations concerned with the issues debated in this book. The descriptions are derived from materials provided by the organizations. All have publications or information available for interested readers. The list was compiled on the date of publication of the present volume; the information provided here may change. Be aware that many organizations take several weeks or longer to respond to inquiries, so allow as much time as possible.

California Nonprofits Student Debt Project

1100 11 St., Suite 10
Sacramento, CA 95814
(800) 776-4226
email: via website form
website: www.calnonprofits.org

The Nonprofit Student Debt Project is a CalNonprofits initiative to educate nonprofit staff and employers, advocate for public policy changes, and educate the community about student debt and its impact on the nonprofit workforce. CalNonprofits is a statewide membership organization that brings nonprofits together for communities throughout California.

The Debt Collective

email: via website form
website: www.debtcollective.org

The Debt Collective is a membership organization that uses the collective power of people in debt (including debt from student loans) to help individuals dispute debt while working for policies to end mass indebtedness, including free college education. The organization's website provides guidance for disputing debt, credit report errors, and lost wages, among other resources.

Freedom to Prosper

email: Contact via website form
website: www.freedomtoprosper.org

Freedom to Prosper is an organization dedicated to ending student debt through education and political action. The group supports forgiveness of student debt and are committed to ensuring access to a tuition-free college education for future generations. Only then, they believe, will the nation be free to prosper.

The Institute for College Access and Success Project on Student Debt

110 Maryland Ave., NE, Suite 201
Washington, DC 20002
(202) 223-6060
website: www.ticas.org

The Institute for College Access and Success is an nonprofit organization working to make college affordable and available for people of all backgrounds. The organization's Project on Student Debt works to lessen the burdens of student debt by improving income-tied repayment plans and strengthening the Pell Grant system.

The Institute on Inequality and Democracy

6249C Public Affairs Building
337 Charles E. Young Drive East
Los Angeles, CA 90095
email: challegeinequality@luskin.ucla.edu
website: www.challengeinequality.luskin.ucla.edu

The Institute on Inequality and Democracy advances radical democracy through research, critical thought, and alliances with social movements and racial justice activism.

Student Aid Alliance

email: Contact via website form
website: www.studentaidalliance.org

The Student Aid Alliance is a coalition of 85 higher education organizations working together to support federal student aid programs, such as the Pell Grant and Work Study programs.

StudentDebtCrisis

(646) 820-8037
email: info@studentdebtcrisis.org
website: www.studentdebtcrisis.org

StudentDebtCrisis is a nonprofit organization that works to change the basic government policies surrounding higher education loans and student debt. The organization shares student loan advocacy, education, and updates with one million supporters. Its website offers student loan tools and other resources to take action.

Student Loan Justice

(234) 567-6757
email: info@studentloanjustice.com
website: www.studentloanjustice.org

Student Loan Justice is a grassroots organization working to help citizens regain the bankruptcy rights and statutes of limitations that are available for other types of loans. The organization recognizes that student loans are not under the same fundamental consumer protections as other types of loans.

United for a Fair Economy

184 High St., Suite 603
Boston, MA 02110-3160
(617) 423-2148
email: jhuezo@faireconomy.org
website: www.faireconomy.org

United for a Fair Economy uses popular economics education, training, and creative communications to support social movements working for a resilient, sustainable and equitable economy.

US Department of Education

400 Maryland Ave., SW
Washington, D.C. 20202
(800) 872-5327
website: www.ed.gov

The official website of the US Department of Education has links to many current resources for understanding and managing student debt.

Bibliography

Books

Beth Akers. *Game of Loans: The Rhetoric and Reality of Student Debt*. Princeton, NJ: Princeton University Press, 2018.

A. J. Angulo. *Diploma Mills: How For-Profit Colleges Stiffed Students, Taxpayers, and the American Dream*. Baltimore, MD: Johns Hopkins University Press, 2016.

Robert B. Archibald and David H. Feldman. *Why Does College Cost so Much?* Oxford, UK: Oxford University Press, 2011.

Elizabeth A. Armstrong and Laura T. Hamilton. *Paying for the Party: How College Maintains Inequality*, Cambridge, MA: Harvard University Press, 2013.

Joel Best and Eric Best. *The Student Loan Mess: How Good Intentions Created a Trillion-Dollar Problem*. Berkeley, CA: University of California Press, 2014.

Heather Boushey, J. Bradford DeLong, and Marshall Steinbaum, eds. *After Piketty: The Agenda for Economics and Inequality*. Cambridge, MA: Harvard University Press, 2017.

Alan Collinge. *The Student Loan Scam: The Most Oppressive Debt in US History and How We Can Fight Back*. Boston, MA: Beacon Press, 2009.

Tressie McMillan Cottom. *Lower Ed: The Troubling Rise of For-Profit Colleges in the New Economy*. New York, NY: New Press, 2018.

William Elliott III and Melinda K. Lewis. *The Real College Debt Crisis: How Student Borrowing Threatens Financial Well-Being and Erodes the American Dream*. Santa Barbara, CA: Praeger, 2015.

Michael Fabricant and Stephen Brier. *Austerity Blues: Fighting for the Soul of Public Higher Education*. Baltimore, MD: Johns Hopkins University Press, 2016.

Sara Goldrick-Rab. *Paying the Price: College Costs, Financial Aid, and the Betrayal of the American Dream*. Chicago, IL: University of Chicago Press, 2016.

Anthony Abraham Jack. *The Privileged Poor: How Elite Colleges Are Failing Disadvantaged Students*. Cambridge, MA: Harvard University Press, 2019.

Cryn Johannsen. *Solving the Student Loan Crisis: Dreams, Diplomas, and a Lifetime of Debt*. Los Angeles, CA: New Insights Press, 2016.

Andrew P. Kelly and Sara Goldrick-Rab, eds. *Reinventing Financial Aid: Charting a New Course to College Affordability*. Cambridge, MA: Harvard Education Press, 2014.

Daniel T. Kirsch. *Sold My Soul for a Student Loan: Higher Education and the Political Economy of the Future*. Santa Barbara, CA: Praeger, 2019.

Christopher P. Loss. *Between Citizens and the State: The Politics of American Higher Education in the 20th Century*. Princeton, NJ: Princeton University Press, 2012.

Walter W. McMahon. *Higher Learning, Greater Good: The Private and Social Benefits of Higher Education*. (Reprint) Baltimore, MD: Johns Hopkins University Press, 2017.

Beth Zasloff. *Hold Fast to Dreams: A College Guidance Counselor, His Students, and the Vision of a Life Beyond Poverty*. New York, NY: New Press, 2014.

Periodicals and Internet Sources

Sabrina Cereceres, "Who's Most Affected by Student Debt? Women." *The Nation*, October 20, 2016. https://www .thenation.com/article/who-is-most-affected-by-student -debt-women/.

Sara Goldrick-Rab, "Public Higher Education Should Be Universal and Free," *The New York Times*, updated January 20, 2016. https://www.nytimes.com/roomfordebate /2016/01/20/should-college-be-free/public-higher -education-should-be-universal-and-free.

Riley Griffen. "The Student Loan Debt Crisis Is about to Get Worse," *Bloomberg*, October 17, 2018. https://www .bloomberg.com/news/articles/2018-10-17/the-student -loan-debt-crisis-is-about-to-get-worse.

Adam Harris, "Another Way Student Debt Keeps People from Buying Homes," *The Atlantic*, July 11, 2018. https://www .theatlantic.com/education/archive/2018/07/another-way -student-debt-keeps-people-from-buying-homes/564860/.

Astead W. Herndon, "Elizabeth Warren's Higher Education Plan: Cancel Student Debt and Eliminate Tuition," *The New York Times*, April 22, 2019. https://www.nytimes .com/2019/04/22/us/politics/elizabeth-warren-student -debt.html.

Richard Hunt, "Proposals for Solving the Federal Student Loan Debt Crisis, *The Tennessean*, April 20, 2019. https://www .tennessean.com/story/opinion/2019/04/21/proposals -solving-student-loan-debt-crisis/3524445002/.

Andrew P. Kelly, "The Problem Is that Free College Isn't Free," *New York Times*, updated January 20, 2016. https://www .nytimes.com/roomfordebate/2016/01/20/should-college -be-free/the-problem-is-that-free-college-isnt-free.

Matt Krupnick, "1.5 Trillion in Student Debt: Student Loan Crisis Shatters a Generation's American Dream," *The*

Guardian, 4 October 2018. https://www.theguardian
.com/money/2018/oct/04/student-loan-crisis-threatens
-a-generations-american-dream.

Sean McElwee, "Promising Signs That America Is Waking Up
to the Student Debt Crisis," *Common Dreams,* April 24,
2019. https://www.commondreams.org/views/2019/04/24
/promising-signs-america-waking-student-debt-crisis.

Amy Merrick, "Should Businesses Help Employees Pay off
Their Student Loans?" *The Atlantic*, May 18, 2018. https://
www.theatlantic.com/education/archive/2018/05/student
-debt/560315/.

Josh Mitchell and Andrea Fuller, "The Student-Debt Crisis
Hits Hardest at Historically Black Colleges," *Wall Street
Journal*, April 17, 2019. https://www.wsj.com/articles
/the-student-debt-crisis-hits-hardest-at-historically-black
-colleges-11555511327.

Lynn Pasquerella, "Higher Education Should Be a Public Good,
Not a Private Commodity," *The Washington Post*, October
20, 2016. https://www.washingtonpost.com/news/in-theory
/wp/2016/10/20/higher-education-should-be-a-public-good
-not-a-private-commodity/?utm_term=.17111dec5dfd.

Anne Helen Petersen, "Here's Why So Many Americans Feel
Cheated by Their Student Loans," *Buzzfeed*, February 9,
2019. https://www.buzzfeednews.com/article
/annehelenpetersen/student-debt-college-public-service
-loan-forgiveness.

Brad Polumbo, "The Student Debt 'Crisis' Is Students' Fault,
and They Shouldn't Get a Bailout," *The Federalist*, March 19,
2018. https://thefederalist.com/2018/03/19/student-debt
-crisis-students-fault-shouldnt-get-bailout/.

Vauhini Vara, "A Student-Debt Revolt Begins," *The New Yorker*,
February 23, 2015. https://www.newyorker.com/business
/currency/student-debt-revolt-begins.

Index

A

American Association of University Women (AAUW), 98, 99, 104, 105, 106, 107, 112

American Student Assistance (ASA), 39, 40

apprenticeships, 58, 59, 115

Australia, 11, 12–13, 14, 15

B

bankruptcy, 8, 26, 36, 60, 63–64

Berliner, Katy, 42, 43

C

cancellation of student debt, 16, 17, 18, 21, 22, 23, 33, 61, 90, 94, 95

capitalism, 88, 89, 99, 100, 102, 107

Chronicle of Higher Education, 103, 116

community colleges, 30, 51, 80, 85–87

Congressional Budget Office, 14, 39

Consumer Financial Protection Bureau (CFPB), 8, 28–29, 61, 62

Council of Economic Advisers (CEA), 78, 82

credit ratings, 9, 12, 18, 19, 35, 36, 37, 91

crowdfunding, 44, 47–49

D

defaulting on loans, 14, 17, 22, 26, 61–62, 65, 79–80, 81, 89, 106

Department of Education, 18, 22, 27, 29, 30, 31, 62, 78, 80, 91, 98

depression, 67, 107

DeVos, Betsy, 27–28, 66

E

economic disadvantages, 19, 21

Economic Policy Institute, 75, 109

education loans, 7–8, 63

England, 11, 13, 15, 93, 96

F

Fair Credit Reporting Act (FCRA), 14

Fair Labor Standards Act (FLSA), 115

Federal Housing Administration (FHA), 14